W9-BCV-527

Identification and Price Guide

MARK F. MORAN

©2004 Krause Publications

Published by

krause publications
An F+W Publications Company

700 East State Street • Iola, WI 54990-0001
715-445-2214 • 888-457-2873
www.krause.com

Our toll-free number to place an order or obtain
a free catalog is (800) 258-0929.

Library of Congress Catalog Number: 2004103288

ISBN: 0-87349-779-1

Edited by Dennis Thornton
Designed by Kay Sanders

Printed in USA

Table Of Contents

A Family Tradition

The first McCoy with clay under his fingernails was W. Nelson McCoy. With his uncle, W.F. McCoy, he founded a pottery works in Putnam, Ohio, in 1848, making stoneware crocks and jugs.

That same year, W. Nelson's son, James W., was born in Zanesville, Ohio. James established the J.W. McCoy Pottery Co. in Roseville, Ohio, in the fall of 1899. The J.W. McCoy plant was destroyed by fire in 1903, and was rebuilt two years later.

It was at this time that the first examples of Loy-Nel-Art wares were produced. The line's distinctive title came from the names of James McCoy's three sons, Lloyd, Nelson, and Arthur. Like other "standard" glazed pieces produced at this time by several Ohio potteries, Loy-Nel-Art has a glossy finish on a dark brown-black body, but Loy-Nel-Art featured a splash of green color on the front, and a burnt-orange splash on the back.

George Brush became general manager of J.W. McCoy Pottery Co. in 1909. The company became Brush-McCoy Pottery Co. in 1911, and in 1925 the name was shortened to Brush Pottery Co. This firm remained in business until 1982.

Separately, in 1910, Nelson McCoy Sr. founded the Nelson McCoy Sanitary and Stoneware Co., also in Roseville. By the early 1930s, production had shifted from utilitarian wares to art pottery, and the company name was changed to Nelson McCoy Pottery.

The Nelson McCoy Pottery Co. in Roseville, Ohio, is shown in a vintage photo, probably from the 1930s.

Designer Sydney Cope was hired in 1934, and was joined by his son, Leslie, in 1936. The Copes' influence on McCoy wares continued until Sydney's death in 1966. That same year, Leslie opened a gallery devoted to his family's design heritage and featuring his own original art.

Nelson McCoy Sr. died in 1945, and was succeeded as company president by his nephew, Nelson McCoy Melick.

A fire destroyed the plant in 1950, but company officials—including Nelson McCoy Jr., then 29—decided to rebuild, and the new Nelson McCoy Pottery Co. was up and running in just six months.

Nelson Melick died in 1954. Nelson Jr. became company president, and oversaw the company's continued growth. In 1967, the operation was sold to entrepreneur David Chase. At this time, the words "Mt. Clemens Pottery" were added to the company marks. In 1974, Chase sold the company to Lancaster Colony Corp., and the company marks included a stylized "LCC" logo. Nelson Jr. and his wife, Billie, who had served as a products supervisor, left the company in 1981.

In 1985, the company was sold again, this time to Designer Accents. The McCoy pottery factory closed in 1990.

The new Nelson McCoy Pottery Co. plant opened after the 1950 fire and operated under various owners until it closed in 1990.

Words of Thanks

This book would not have been possible without the help and good wishes of the following:

Carol Seman and Dan Eggert of Brecksville, Ohio. Carol publishes the NM Xpress newsletter, and can be reached at http://www.members.aol.com/nmxpress/

John and Polly Sweetman of Townsend, Del., whose Web site is http://www.mccoylovers.com/mcgoldtrim/

Kathleen Moloney of New York, N.Y.

Pat and Royal Ritchey of Cullman, Ala.

Basil and Dianna Atkins, Ohio

Janel Schultz of Winona, Minn.

Rose Kowles of Winona, Minn

A fire destroyed the McCoy factory in 1950, but the plant was rebuilt and was operating again in six months.

Workers inspect the burned-out remains of the McCoy pottery factory.

To Begin With ...

This book does not contain every single piece of McCoy pottery. No book does, and perhaps no single book could. The variety and volume of wares produced by the several incarnations of McCoy potteries during more than 14 decades are staggering, and previously unknown or experimental pieces are still being found today. But thanks to a generous and devoted group of collectors willing to share their time and treasures, this volume presents a detailed view of the products of an American institution.

Cookie Jars

Cookie jars represent one of most popular categories for McCoy collectors. Even the most enthusiastic collectors admit that the McCoy lid designs and configurations contribute to the dings and cracks common on these pieces, so condition is an important consideration. Many jars also have cold-paint decoration (done by hand on top of the glazed surfaces) and this paint is easily worn. Examples with good paint bring a premium price. This category has also been plagued by fakes.

Two Apple jars. Red example is late 1950s, McCoy USA mark, and same form as Blushing Apple jar, but is cold painted with gold finial. **$75-$85**

White Apple jar, nicknamed "The Tooth," has a leaf lid found on other fruit-form jars, early 1970s, McCoy USA mark. **$50-$60**

Apollo jar with original paper flag and label, 1970-71, McCoy mark. **$350-$400**

Two variations of **Apple jars:** the first, as it came from the factory without leaf knob; second, flat-leaf apple with strong burgundy and yellow glaze.

Cookie Jars

Asparagus jar, 1970s. **$75-$85**

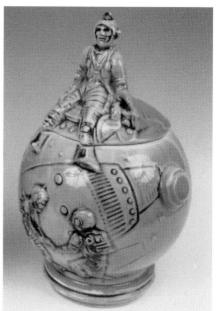

Astronaut jar, 1960s, USA mark. **$350-$400** (Rarely in dark blue.)

Hand-painted ball jar with slanted knob (also comes with rectangular knob), stoneware, late 1930s to early 1950s, unmarked. **$45-$55,** depending on paint condition. (This shape was reissued in the mid-1960s.)

Ball jar in cobalt blue, 1940s, unmarked, 6 1/2" tall. **$90-$110**

Two versions of the **Banana jar,** 1948, McCoy mark. Left is the more typical glaze. **$200-$250,** depending on color; often found with damage to lid points.

Barn jar with cow in door, 1960s, McCoy USA mark, lid was easily damaged. **$350-$400**

Baseball Boy and Football Boy jars, late 1970s to early '80s, McCoy USA mark. **$175-$225 each,** with the Baseball Boy in the higher range. Beware of reproductions.

Two **Basket-weave jars,** late 1950s, McCoy USA mark, one topped with apples, the other with pears. The word "Cookies" was cold-painted and is often worn; often found with damage to fruit. **$100-$125 each**

Two **Basket-weave jars,** late 1950s, McCoy USA mark, one topped with pine cones, the other with a puppy. The word "Cookies" was cold-painted and is often worn; often found with damage to lids. **$100-$125 each**

Two versions of the **Bear with Cookie in Vest.** At left is an unusual color combination with cold-painted lid. **$350-$450**

Right, jar has cold-paint trim on white. **$90-$110** (Originally from the mid-1940s, this jar was also made in the 1950s with the word "Cookies" between the bear's feet.)

Reproduction **Bear with Cookie in Vest,** left, next to the original. New jar is shorter at 9 3/4" and much lighter than original and was not made by McCoy, despite having an impressed McCoy mark on the base.

Big Orange jar, early 1970s, McCoy USA mark, cold-painted stem and leaves. **$90-$110**

Two **Blushing Apple jars**, 1950s and '60s, McCoy USA mark. Example at left has leaf finial in wrong position. Typically about **$75**. With misplaced finial, **$100**. (Rarely found with saw-tooth leaf on lid.)

Left, **Bobby Baker jar,** 1970s, McCoy USA mark, also comes in lower flat hat. **$50-$60** Right, **Betsy Baker,** 1970s, McCoy USA mark, also comes in ruffled hat. **$175-$225** With rare rounded hat with button top, called "Betty Baker." **$300+**

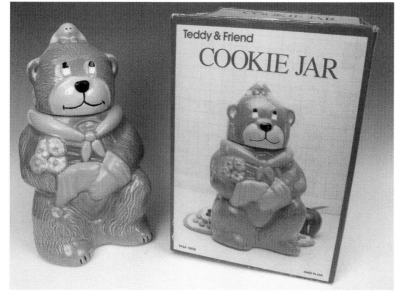

Above left, **Bubbles the Pig jar/bank** with original box, late 1970s, McCoy USA mark; Left, **Teddy and Friend** in factory glazes with original box; Above, **Chilly Willy** in factory glazes with original box. **$75-$100 each**

Cookie Jars

Left, reproduction **Cauliflower Mammy jar. $25-$30** Right, real Cauliflower Mammy jar with expected worn cold paint. **$500-$600** (Prices for this jar once hovered around $1,000, but the reproductions have driven values down.)

The following is from NM Xpress (http://www.members.aol.com/nmxpress/), Carol Seman and Dan Eggert, Brecksville, Ohio: Chairman of the Board: The Chairman of the Board jar was produced in 1985. It was designed during the brief time that Lancaster Colony owned McCoy. It came in two versions: maroon and brown pants. Both the original and reproduction are marked 162-USA. The original Chairman stands 10 5/8" tall and the reproduction is 9 3/4" tall. Once again, height can help you determine the authenticity of this cookie jar.

Chef, 1960s, McCoy USA mark. **$175-$200** Found with blue face and other scarf colors. (Beware of reproductions shorter than 11".)

Chilly Willy holiday variation, hand-painted at home in Christmas colors by a McCoy employee, late 1980s, USA mark. Because of paint, **$175-$225** Normally, **$75-$100**

Chairman of the Board in maroon pants (he also comes with brown pants), 1985, marked 162-USA. **$400-$500**

Chipmunk jar, early 1960s, McCoy USA mark. **$100-$125** (This is easily distinguished from the rare and expensive Squirrel jar—sometimes called Fox Squirrel—which has a much larger tail and is valued at about $4,000.)

Two versions of **Clown in a Barrel jar,** mid-1950s, McCoy USA mark, cold-painted details. **$100-$125**

Circus Horse with Monkey jar, 1961, McCoy USA mark, cold-painted details, easily damaged. **$150-$200**

Two versions of **Clown in a Barrel,** mid-1950s, McCoy USA mark, cold-painted details. **$100-$125**

Clyde the Dog jar, mid-1970s, McCoy USA LCC mark, cold-painted details. **$250-$300**

Two versions of **Clown in a Barrel,** mid-1950s, McCoy USA mark, cold-painted details on all white example, all green example is rare. **$400-$500 each**

Cookie Jars

Left, **Cookie Bank** (modeled on the actual Main Street bank building in Roseville, Ohio), with money slot on reverse, 1960s, McCoy Bank mark.
Right, **Cookie Cabin,** 1950s, unmarked, with cold-painted details.
$90-$110 each

Cookie Box (also called the Jewel Box), 1963, USA mark.
$150-$175

Cookie Boy jar in turquoise with crisp mold detail, early 1940s, McCoy mark. **$300-$350** (Rarely found bare headed.)

Cookie Boy jars in yellow and white, early 1940s, McCoy mark. **$200-$225 each**

Two **cookie jars** in gold trim, late 1940s to '50s. **Sack of Cookies** has McCoy USA mark, other jar unmarked. **$40-$50 each**

Cookie Special jar, early 1960s, McCoy USA mark, cold-painted details. **$125-$175**

Cookie Tug jar with cold-paint decoration, 1950s, McCoy USA mark. **$8,000-$10,000**

Left, **Cookie Wagon** (also called the "Conestoga Wagon"), 1960s, McCoy USA mark, with glaze and cold paint. **$75-$90**
Right, **Cookie House,** late 1950s, McCoy USA mark, with split roof lid, easily damaged, with glaze and cold paint. **$125-$140**

Cork crock jar, 1975, McCoy USA mark, can be hard to find complete because lid often broke. **$90-$110**

Down on the Farm Cow, early 1990s, Designer Accents mark. **$90-$110**
(Not to be confused with the rare Reclining Cow—also known as "Cookies and Milk Cow"—which sold at auction for $10,000.)

Dalmatians in Rocking Chair, early 1960s, McCoy USA Dalmatians mark. **$325-$375** (Beware of reproductions shorter than 9".

The following is from NM Xpress (http://www.members.aol.com/nmxpress/), Carol Seman and Dan Eggert, Brecksville, Ohio:

Davy Crockett: Made by McCoy in 1957, the original Davy jar is 10 1/4" tall and is marked USA on the bottom. In 1994, reproductions of Davy Crockett surfaced, believed to have their origin in Ohio. The reproductions are marked the same (USA) but they don□t measure up. The reproduction is barely 9 1/2" tall, making height a good way to tell whether or not it is "the real McCoy!"

Left, reproduction **Davy Crockett jar;** right, original Crockett jar, late 1950s, USA mark, all decoration under glaze. **$450-$550** (Prices for this jar once hovered around $700, but the reproductions have driven values down.)

Two versions of **Doghouse with Bird jar,** left being more common, 1980s, later reissued by Lancaster Colony. **$175-$200**
(The same dog and bird forms on the front of the jar were found on a rare pair of bookends—possibly for sales samples—that sold at auction for $4,000.)

Two versions of the **Drum jar,** 1960, McCoy USA mark, all cold-painted so examples may be found nearly white. Red, white, and blue is more common than brown and yellow. **$90-$110 each**

Duck on Basket-weave, 1950s, McCoy USA mark, cold-painted details. **$90-$110**

Two versions of the **Elephant jar,** both with cold-painted details. Example at left is called "split trunk" and is harder to find, 1940s, unmarked. **$275-$300**
Example at right has complete trunk as part of lid, 1950s, unmarked. **$150-$175**

Engine jar, early 1960s, McCoy USA mark, cold-painted details. **$125-$175,** with other color combinations found on engine.

Two other color combinations for **Engine jar. $250-$300 each**

Fireplace lamp and cookie jar made from the same mold, late 1960s, USA mark. **$75-$100** for the jar, **$125-$150** for the lamp (rare).

Forbidden Fruit jar, late 1960s, McCoy USA mark, with cold paint on the lid. **$90-$110**

Flat-leaf Apple cookie jar, glossy maroon, 1930s. **$125-$150**

Flowerpot jar, 1960s, flower forms vary and can be replaced. **$200-$225**

Freddie the Gleep, mid-1970s, cold-paint details (also available in lime green), has been reproduced slightly smaller, 10 1/4". **$350-$400**

Friendship 7 jar, 1960s, unmarked, cold-paint details. **$100-$125**

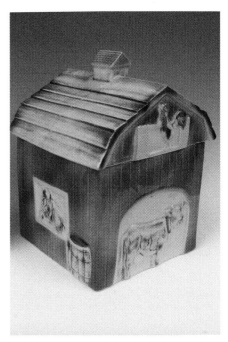

Barn jar with cow in door, 1960s, McCoy USA mark, lid was easily damaged. **$350-$400**

Globe jar, cold-painted details, 1960, McCoy USA mark. **$250-$300**

Granny with Glasses jar, on the left is the model used to make molds, and the production jar is at right, 1970s, USA mark. **$90-$110** Also found in white with gold trim.

Grapes jar with bird on lid in air-brushed colors, non-production piece, McCoy mark, 9 1/2" tall. **$7,000+**

Hamm's Bear jar, early 1970s, USA mark, also found with white tie. **$225-$250**

Harley Hog bank, 1984, HD McCoy mark but not made by McCoy, also found with decal and contrasting cap. **$90-$110**

Hen on Nest, late 1950s, USA mark, cold-painted details. **$90-$110**

Hobnail jars, stoneware, in yellow and hard-to-find cobalt, early 1940s, unmarked, note difference in lid configurations. **$100-$125 each**

Hobnail jars, stoneware, in blue and hard-to-find coral, early 1940s, unmarked. **$100-$125 each**

Two **Hobnail Heart jars,** in pale yellow and blue, early 1940s, unmarked. **$300-$350 each**

Two **Hobnail Heart jars** in streaky blue and pink, early 1940s, unmarked. **$300-$350 each**

Two **Hobnail Heart jars** in matte white and lavender, early 1940s, unmarked. **$300-$350 each**

Hocus Rabbit jar, late 1970s, also found in gray, and may be marked "McCoy USA LCC" or with Designer Accents logo. **$80-$90**

Honey Bear jar with all decoration under glaze (some examples have cold paint), 1950s, McCoy USA mark. **$75-$90** for glazed, **$110-$125** for good cold paint.

Indian jar with cold-paint decoration, 1950s, McCoy mark 11 1/2". **$200-$225**
At right is a model of the Indian jar, which was used to make a block from which the mold was cast.

Two commemorative **Indian jars** from the 1990s (slightly smaller than the originals), made by George Williams. Rick Wisecarver of Roseville, Ohio, painted the one on the right.
Left, **$150-$200**
Right, **$450-$550**

Jack-o'-Lantern jar, also comes with orange lid, late 1950s, McCoy USA mark. **$550-$650**

Left, **Joey Kangaroo jar,** late 1950s, McCoy USA mark. **$300-$350**
Right, **Blue Kangaroo,** mid-1960s, USA mark. **$225-$250**

Kissing Penguins or Lovebirds, in typical factory cold paint decoration, 1940s, McCoy mark. **$90-$110** (Rarely found in brown and green.)

Left, **Kittens on a Basket,** 1950s, McCoy USA mark, cold-painted details, seldom found without damage to ears, so beware of restorations. **$450-$550**
Right, **Kitten on Coal Bucket,** 1983, McCoy USA LCC mark, also found with brown kitten on black bucket. **$200-$250**

Koala jar, 1980s, McCoy USA LCC mark. **$125-$150**

Lamb on Basket-weave, 1950s, McCoy USA mark, cold-painted details. **$90-$110**

Lamb on Cylinder, 1950s, McCoy USA mark, cold-painted details. **$200-$225** (Also found with cats and dogs on lid.)

Lamb on Basket-Weave jar in atypical golden, green, and burgundy, 1950s, McCoy USA mark, all decoration under glaze. **$400-500**

Lemon jar, 1970s. **$75-$85**

Liberty Bell jar, 1960s, unmarked, more common in silver than in bronze. **$75-$90**

Little Clown jar, mid-1940s, McCoy mark, cold-painted details. **$80-$100**

Lollipop jar, late 1950s, McCoy USA mark, cold painted. **$70-$80**

Lunchbox jar, late 1980s, marked Designer Accents #377 USA. **$40-$50** (Rarely found with green lid.)

Cookie Jars

The following is from NM Xpress (http://www.members.aol.com/nmxpress/), Carol Seman and Dan Eggert, Brecksville, Ohio:

McCoy Mammy: Original Mammy is a full 11" tall and comes in white, yellow, and aqua. The bottom is marked McCoy and is glazed with a dry foot. Details on some examples are cold painted on top of the glaze and show much wear. The reproduction jar is 10 1/4" tall, noticeably smaller all around. Unfortunately, it is marked the same and the cold-painted details can be scratched to look as if it has aged. Height is the best indicator to help authenticate the jar.

Left, reproduction **Mammy jar**; right, real Mammy jar with checked apron (paint touched up).

Mammy jar in yellow, also found in white and aqua with cold paint decoration (widely available as a slightly smaller reproduction), 1950s, McCoy mark. **$200-$225**
(Rarely found with two other phrases around base: "Dem Cookies Sure Am Good" and "Dem Cookies Sho Got Dat Vitamin A."

Mother Goose, late 1940s, McCoy USA mark, cold-painted details. **$90-$110**

A **1999 Nelson McCoy Pottery Company jar,** made in Crooksville, Ohio, as a commemorative, only 500 made. **$300-$350**

Nabisco jar, 1974, McCoy USA mark. **$70-$100**

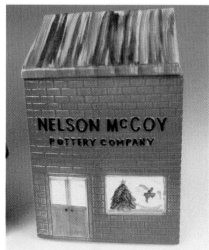

Nursery Rhyme canister jars, early 1970s, unmarked, including Baa Baa Black Sheep, Humpty Dumpty, Little Bo Peep, Little Boy Blue, Little Miss Muffet, and Mary Mary Quite Contrary. **$75-$100 each**

Oak Leaf and Acorn corner jar (previously thought to have been produced by American Bisque), 1948, McCoy mark. **$200-$225**

Mr. and Mrs. Owl jar, 1950s, McCoy USA mark, cold-painted details. **$90-$110**

Peanut Bird jar, late 1970s, unmarked. **$150-$175**

Two versions of the **Pear jar,** both 1950s. The shorter jar on the left has pale yellow glaze and cold-painted leaves and stem. **$100-$125 each**

Two more variations of the **Pear jar.** First, a blushing example with strong glaze on leaf knob and minimal burgundy glaze. Second, a flat-leaf pear with strong burgundy and yellow glaze.

A yellow and green **Pear jar,** 1950s, seen here with damage. Without damage, **$125-$150**

Lunch-hour piece, a **Pear jar** with a cat finial that was intended for use on a planter called "Pussy at the Well," 1950s. **$850-$1,000**

Penguin jar, early 1940s, McCoy mark, typically found with worn cold paint, also found in yellow and pale green glaze. **$125-$150,** depending on paint condition.

Two **Pepper jars** in yellow and green, early 1970s to about 1980, either McCoy or McCoy USA marks, lids are not interchangeable, rarely found with textured glaze. **$45-$50 each**

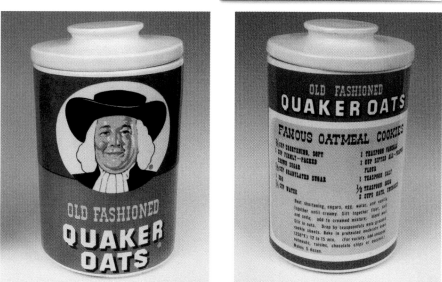

Picnic Basket jar, early 1960s, USA mark, with cold paint on the lid, 1960s. **$90-$110**

Quaker Oats jar, 1970, unmarked, not many McCoy examples, jar was later made by another company. **$500-$600**

"Quigley" jar, also known as Lazy Pig, mid 1980s, USA mark, with original box. **$75-$100**

Pink Pig jar/bank, late 1970s, McCoy USA mark. **$90-$110**

Two versions of the **Raggedy Ann jar,** 1970s, USA mark. Left is painted with typical factory colors, right was hand-painted by a McCoy employee. **$90-$110** for factory colors

Cookie Jars

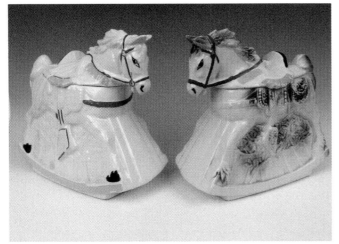

Two versions of the **Rocking Horse jar,** 1950, McCoy USA mark. Cold-painted example on left is harder to find than glazed green and brown. **$150-$175 each**

Two versions of the **Rooster jar**, late 1950s to mid-'60s, McCoy USA mark. Blue-gray is harder to find. **$150-$175 each**

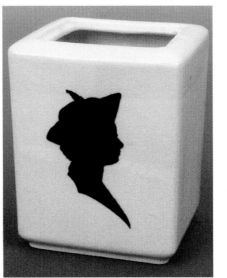

Sad Clown jar, early 1970s, unmarked, cold-painted details. **$90-$110**

Two views of a non-production **Silhouette cookie jar** with images of boy and girl hand-painted under the glaze (normally this form would have floral decoration), 1950s, missing lid, 6 1/2" tall. **No established value.**

Single Ear of Corn, 1958, McCoy USA mark, with good color match in the glaze, and with original label. **$125-$150**

Snow Bear jar, 1960s, McCoy USA mark, with cold-painted details. **$75-$85**

Cookie Jars

Stagecoach jar, also comes in white with gold trim, hard to find, and paint wear affects value only slightly. **$700-$800**

Strawberries in a Basket, hard to find undamaged, late 1970s. **$150-$200**

Strawberry jar, 1950s, McCoy USA mark. **$80-$100**

Teddy and Friend holiday variation, hand-painted at home in Christmas colors by a McCoy employee, late 1980s. Because of paint, **$175-$225** Normally, **$75-$100**

Left, reproduction **Tepee jar;** right, original Tepee jar, late 1950s, McCoy USA mark, straight top, cold-paint decoration, 11" tall. **$250-$300**

Two styles of the **Tepee jar,** late 1950s, McCoy USA mark, slant top (left) and straight top, cold-paint decoration, 11" tall. **$275-$325** for slant top

Thinking Puppy, late 1970s, USA mark, **$40-$50** (Rarely found in tan or yellow.)

Touring Car jar in rare all black with gold trim, early 1960s, McCoy USA mark. **$200-$225**

Tulip Flowerpot jar, late 1950s, McCoy USA mark, found in other color combinations. **$125-$150**

Touring Car in more common black and white with cold-painted details. **$100-$125**

Two versions of the **Turkey jar,** first made mid-1940s, later in about 1960, brown with cold-painted wattle is more common. **$175-$200** Green glaze is harder to find and has no cold paint. **$250-$300** (Look for variations in label around turkey's neck.)

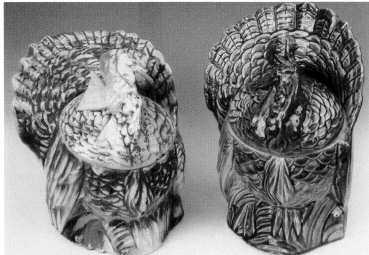

Left, **Turkey jar** in white with all cold-paint decoration, 1940s. **$250-$300,** depending on paint condition. Right, **McCoy Limited Turkey bell** (part of a set of seven with varying motifs), 1990s. **$70-$80**

Uncle Sam's Hat, mid-1970s, unmarked, hard to find. **$700-$800**

W.C. Fields jar, 1972, USA mark. **$200-$250**

Wedding jar, 1960s, McCoy USA mark. **$90-$110**

Windmill jar, 1961, McCoy USA mark, note color variation between lid and jar. **$70-$110,** depending on color match

Two versions of the **Winking Pig jar,** early 1970s, USA mark, typically found with cold-painted details. Yellow example is unusual. **$200-$250**

Wishing Well jar, 1960s, McCoy USA mark. **$50-$60**

Woodsy Owl jar and bank, 1970s, USA mark on jar, cold-painted details. Jar, **$250-$300;** Bank, **$90-$110**

Wren House jar with "V" top, in an atypical realistic glaze, early 1960s, McCoy USA mark, 9 1/2" tall. As shown with V top, **$1,800-$2,000**; "V" top in normal colors, **$600-$700**

Collection Features
Rare McCoy Cookie Jars

All the jars assembled are McCoy, from the collection of Kathleen Moloney of New York City.

The following is from NM Xpress (http://www.members.aol.com/nmxpress/), Carol Seman and Dan Eggert, Brecksville, Ohio:

McCoy cookie jar collectors have known for a long time that there is at least one Tony Veller cookie jar. A photograph of the piece—in solid green—rates a full page in Volume 1 of Joyce Roerig's *Collector's Encyclopedia of Cookie Jars*. The same jar is pictured on page 67 of Sanfords *Guide to McCoy Pottery*. But now we know there's a second Tony Veller, and it's quite different from the first. Hand-finished and lavishly decorated by Sidney Cope himself, it appears to be a prototype. It's also an obvious companion to the original Barge Lady cookie jar in the Cope Gallery.

The jar is 10 1/2" tall and marked NM. The painstakingly detailed and colorful decorations, easily recognizable as the work of Sidney Cope, are under the glaze. As you can see from the picture, this version says "Cookies" on the sack, while Joyce Roerig's says "Tony Veller." What you probably cannot make out is how sharp some of the edges are. (If you're not careful, you could actually cut yourself on the brim of Tony's hat.) Because the jar was finished by hand when it was green ware, many of its details are rough. The foundation that Tony stands on is unusually high, and the rim of the base is quite thick—strong indications that this is indeed a prototype.

According to Leslie Cope, this jar came right out of the Cope gallery. It was given (or possibly sold) by Sidney Cope to family friend Norris F. Schneider. In time, Schneider passed Tony along to a Weller collector, who sold it in October 1998 to a dealer in Roseville, Ohio.

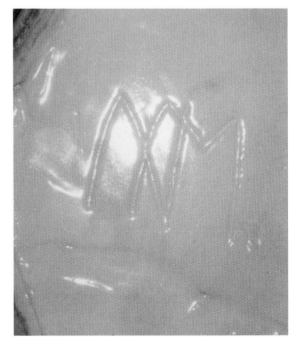

Tony Veller: Probably the most highly prized of all McCoy cookie jars. **$10,000 plus**

Leprechaun: Five versions of a rare jar. It was not produced, but unfortunately it has been reproduced. **$2,000-$5,000 depending on color**

Bareheaded Cookie Boy: Two versions of a rare jar, never produced. (The expressions on the boys' faces are quite different.) **$4,000+**

It's a fairly well-known fact that the Bareheaded Cookie Boy, one of the most sought after of all the non-production McCoy cookie jars, came in different colors. Of the four examples known to exist, three are yellow, and one is green. (There must be a white one out there somewhere.) Attentive readers of reference books might also be aware that the hatless lad was given a couple of different expressions by design-er Sidney Cope. As you can see in the accompanying picture, the little guy on the left (who is yellow) has a sweet, innocent smile. His buddy (green) looks mischievous, even mean. We've recently discovered yet another variable among the BCBs, and that is height. The devilish looking boy on the left is 9" tall. His friendlier brother measures 8 3/4".

McCoy Pottery | *Warmans*

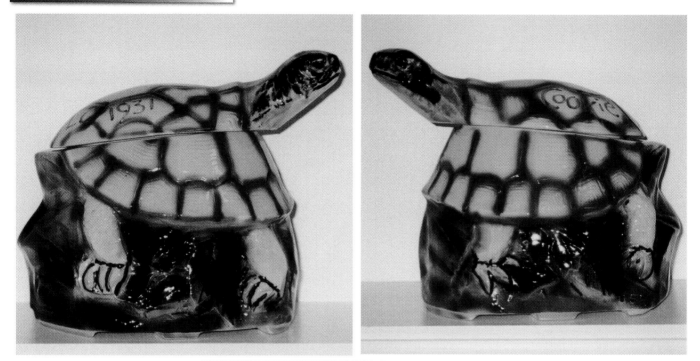

Turtle: This jar was never produced either, and we only know of two of them for sure. For a while, there was some question that it was made by McCoy. Recently, though, an original Cope sketch of the jar was discovered at the Cope Gallery. Mystery solved. **$7,500**

Fox Squirrel: Four versions of a rare jar. It's not as rare as we once thought, but it's pretty hard to find. The two hand-painted ones shown are painted over the glaze. There is one in the Cope Gallery with paint under the glaze.

Two squirrel jars. **$500-$3,500 each**

Is there any such thing as a one-of-a-kind cookie jar? Probably not.

A wise man (Gerald Donaldson of Crooksville, Ohio) once said, "If they made one, they probably made six. If they made six, they probably made twelve." When Gerald shared those pearls of wisdom, he was educating a couple of rookie collectors about the McCoy Fox Squirrel, but he could just as easily have been referring to several other rare McCoy jars. For years, cookie jar collectors were given to understand that there was just one Reclining Cow, one Tugboat, one Tony Veller, one Carousel, one Bareheaded Cookie Boy, and one Basketball. Today we know there are at least two Cows, two Tugboats, two Tony Vellers, two Carousels, and a minimum of three Basketballs. We've located four Bareheaded Cookie Boys. The Fox Squirrel? It turns out there are at least 12.

The Fox Squirrel—sometimes called the Red Squirrel—has always been one of the most coveted of all McCoy cookie jars. People talk a lot about the Hillbilly Bear (or at least they did until the reproduction came out), but they covet the Fox Squirrel, maybe because they know they have a fighting chance of finding one. If you've seen the Squirrel, you know why it appears prominently on so many collectors' want lists. For one thing, its meticulous design, and brown and green decoration, are pure McCoy. There's no way you could mistake it for anything else. For another, it's one of the best looking of all the McCoy cookie jars. To top it off, there's the very appeal-

ing matter of the Squirrel's scarcity. We all want what we can't have.

As luck would have it, one collector had a chance to add a Fox Squirrel to his or her collection in July of 2003, at Jeff Koehler's Pottery Week auction in Crooksville, Ohio. The sale included, among other things, some great Brush, Weller, Watt, and McCoy pieces. But for cookie jar collectors, the piece de resistance was, no contest, a white Squirrel cookie jar decorated with cold paint. Until news of the auction began to spread and flyers were mailed out, nobody even knew that there was such a thing. The only non-brown Squirrel that people knew about was the white Squirrel decorated with paint under the glaze. The real thing, a wonder to behold, is on display in the Cope Gallery.

So the auction was, for many reasons, a very big deal. It ran for many hours, but the white Squirrel was sold in the first 10 minutes, which spared at least four bidders a trip to the nearest emergency room. The final bid—$3,500—brought a round of applause.

Back in June of 2003, when we first learned that a Squirrel would be auctioned during Pottery Week, someone had an idea. Why don't we ask collectors to bring their Squirrel cookie jars to Zanesville with them? Imagine a whole gang of Squirrel cookie jars sitting on a table. Talk about a photo opportunity!

The gathering of seven Squirrel jars in the early morning before the Koehler auction was more than just a photo op. It was also an educational experience, even for the long-time collectors who own them. It was no surprise to discover that there are differences among the various Squirrels. These jars were produced as samples, so naturally the decorators experimented with different colors. The real surprise was how much they differ one from another. Some are light brown with a lot of bright green. Others are darker brown or redder, with very little green. Two of the seven are a dark brown—almost the color of root beer—with no green at all. And the two white Squirrels, one with paint under glaze and the other with cold paint, are sweet variations on the same theme.

Nearly all of the jars came from private collections in the Zanesville area in the last 10 years. Collectors tracked them down and bought them from local residents or other collectors.

Fox Squirrel cookie jars—like all McCoy cookie jars that did not make their way into production—don't usually come cheap. The lowest price we heard about was a staggering $500, and the highest was $3,900. Two of the jars cost $3,500 apiece. The rest were between $1,000 and $2,800.

Dem Cookies Mammy: There are many variations of the Mammy cookie jar (you can see several colors in my group shot). This one is the most sought after of all, because along the base it says, "Dem Cookies sho got dat Vitamin A." This version was not produced. This one, in a matte aqua, is supposedly one of only two in existence. **$4,000**

Pine Cones: The base is the same as Mr. and Mrs. Owl jar, but the lid was an experiment. It was not produced and is possibly one of a kind. One side says Cookies, the other "When Shadows Fall." **$2,500**

Blue Train: This one was designed in 1986 but was never produced. There are a couple versions in red and at least one in gray, but this may be the only one that was done in blue. **$2,500**

Indian: The one on the left is hard to find. The one on the right is possibly one of a kind. It looks very like the one on the left, but it's different, mostly because it does not have the word "Cookies" on the base. Supposedly the non-Cookies version was produced as a prototype. **Left, $200. Right, $3,000**

Apple: A common jar in a very unusual glaze. **$250**

Forbidden Fruit: A common jar in a very unusual glaze. **$300**

Even the most enthusiastic collector will admit that some of the cookie jars McCoy made were a little—how can we put this nicely?—boring. The canisters are pretty dull, of course. So are the Cookstoves and the Teapots and the Churn. Another jar that's not exactly in the Top 10 is the Keebler Tree.

But wait. That Keebler jar is a lot more interesting than you think.

Produced by Nelson McCoy (a Lancaster Colony Company) from 1986 to 1991, the Keebler Tree you see at flea markets today is not quite the jar that McCoy started out to make. The original McCoy jar did not include decals. In the beginning, the Keebler elf and the Keebler sign were incorporated into the mold and painted by hand. (That's how the Keebler jars produced by Haeger were designed. McCoy based its mold on Haeger's when it took over the Keebler contract.)

Keebler Treehouse: This is the earliest version, with applied (three-dimensional) decorations, not decals. The version that was mass-produced had decals. **$250**

Why the change? According to a McCoy employee who spent a day decorating the first Keeblers produced by McCoy, painting the elf and the sign by hand just took too long. She decorated 16 to 18 jars during her shift—not enough to satisfy the supervisors at the plant. So, for the sake of efficiency, the elf and the sign were simply scraped off the mold and replaced by decals. It was too late to change the catalog, though. The three-dimensional Keebler Tree is pictured on the cover of the 1986 cookie jar catalog (item #0350-0573). The 3-D Keebler is immortalized on the box as well.

The bottom line for collectors is that at least a few of those 16 to 18 early McCoy Keebler Trees have to be out there somewhere, and they're definitely not boring. They're 9 1/2" high, 7" wide at the base, with the flat, unglazed bottom you expect from a sample. The Haeger jar is about an inch bigger all around with a fully glazed brown bottom.

Flowerpot with Tulip: This comes in red and yellow versions. As you can see, there is also a variation in the tulip finial. **$200**

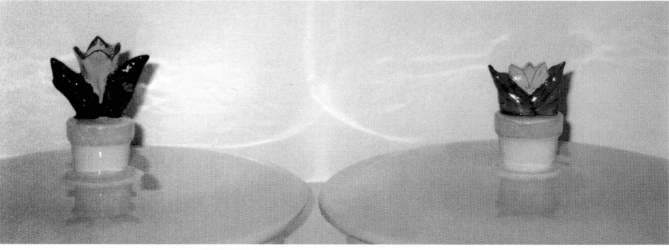

White Turkey: There are three versions of the Turkey, multicolored, green, and white—all of them uncommon but mass produced. This one is pictured because it has been hand-decorated under the glaze. Decorators at the factory did this once in a while, as a gift for a family member or friend. This one appears to say, "The Lasiters." The decorated Football Boy is another good example of these lunch hour specials. **$300**

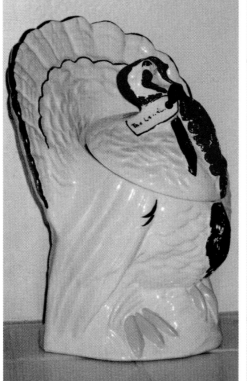

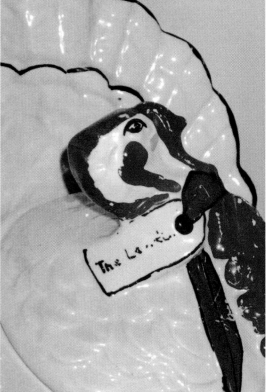

Football Boy: The standard Football Boy is pictured on the right. The one on the left has been customized, with the colors of the Crooksville Ceramics, and the name and number (on the back) of one of the players. There are others of these around in different school colors. **Left, $500. Above, $150 each.**

The Koala: The standard (and fairly common) Koala is on the left. The one on the right is marked "Sample" on the bottom and is done in an unusual glaze. **Standard glaze, $100, Atypical glaze, $300**

Kissing Penguins: The standard jar (which is also called Lovebirds) is on the right. There are several unusual color variations out there, including one in a variegated green. This one is solid black. **Left, $1,000, Right, $100**

Cat on a Coal Bucket: There are two versions of the jar, produced but not terribly common. **$200-$250**

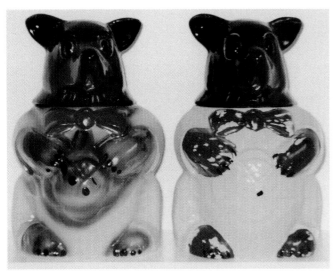

Flowerpot with Plastic Flowers: It was produced, but it's pretty rare. Sometimes you see one with obviously replaced flowers. **$200+**

Bear with Cookies in Vest: The most common version of this not hard-to-find jar is glazed white and decorated with cold paint. In this picture, the one on the right is yellow and decorated mostly with cold paint over the glaze. The decorations on the Bear on the left are almost all under glaze. Both are pretty hard to come by. **$250-$450 each**

Cookie House: A popular jar, along with the two others in the "set": the Bank and the Cabin. **$200+**

Cookie Bank and Cookie Cabin

 The McCoy Cookie Bank cookie jar was created in the image of a real bank, and it's right on Main Street in Roseville, Ohio. When Leslie Cope designed the jar, produced in 1961 and usually considered one of a set of three, along with the Cookie Cabin and Cookie House, he used this local bank as a model. **$90-$110 each**

Christmas Tree: The two versions: one silver, one gold. They were produced but are not easy to find. It's very popular. **$750-$1,000 each**

Rooster: The two versions, both produced. **$75 each**

Hobnail Heart: Simple and unadorned but very highly valued jars. These are the standard five colors. **$300-$350 each**

Grandfather Clock: The simple brown on the right is the easiest to find of the three. On the left, you have the butterscotch covered (partially) with silver. In the center is green. **$200+ each**

Jack-o'-Lantern: The one with the green top is marginally rarer and more popular than the other. **$550-$650 each**

Penguin: The three colors. **$125-$150 each**

Wren House: The one on the far left has a "split top." It's far more rare and sought after than the other two. **Left, $1,800-$2000. Others, $600-$700**

Stagecoach: The one on the left and the one on the right are the same except for the decorations. The one on the right is decorated completely under glaze, while the one on the left has some cold paint. The one in the center was made from a different mold. It is generally thought to be McCoy, but we're not sure. **$700-$800 each**

Cookie Jars

Train Engine and Caboose: The first photo shows four versions of the engine: in butterscotch, decorated black, decorated yellow, and butterscotch overlaid with silver. More are shown below. **$125-$300 each**

Basketball: Last but definitely not least, this is a jar that was not produced. There are at least three around (remember, if they made one, they probably made six; if they made six, they probably made 12), each is decorated very differently. **$4,000**

| 0143-4673 Bear and Bee Hive | 0141-0873 Panda Bear | 0142-8873 Bear and Barrell | 0162-8800 Chairman of the Board |
| 0204-4A73 Owl Rattan | 0272-4A73 Hound Dog Rattan | 0353-4A73 Hot Air Balloon Red Stripes | 0159-0873 Ice Cream Cone |

A Panda Bear jar highlighted this group of eight McCoy cookie jars in an undated promotion.

HODGE PODGE II

The Nelson McCoy Pottery Company
Roseville, Ohio 43777
Subsidiary of Lancaster Colony Corp.

22-0247-11
11" x 6"
Contemporary Cookie Jar,

22-0221-15
Liberty Bell Cracker Jar,

27-7527-53
10" x 11"
Blue Antique Pitcher
& Bowl,

22-0196-53
11" x 7"
Rancher Cookie Jar,

28-0299-53
12oz. Mug,

22-0184-73
11" x 7"
Betty Baker Cookie Jar,

22-0219-46
8" x 6¾" Owl Cookie Jar,

Several jars, including a Liberty Bell Cracker Jar, were featured in McCoy's "Hodge Podge II" collection.

Hand Crafted Cookie Jars

22-0156-73

22-0201-73

WOODSY OWL

Assortment 22-0173-55

22-0202-11

The Nelson McCoy Pottery Company
Roseville, Ohio 43777

22-0846-38

22-0848-38

TIME FOR COOKIES

Assortment 22-0117-55

DUTCH TREAT

22-0847-38

22-7019-16

Kookie Kettle

22-0171-04

cookie pot

Assortment 22-0168-55

22-0220-11

Page 3

Several cookie jars, including Woodsy Owl, a monk, and a Kookie Kettle, were featured in the 1973 McCoy catalog.

Cookie Jars

Hand Decorated Ceramic Cookie Jars

HAND DECORATED Cookie Jar

180 - Wishing Well

187 - Wind Mill

182 - Caboose

181 - Wedding Jar

179 - Coffee Grinder

178 - Oaken Bucket

184 - Pitcher

186 - Sack of Cookies

185 - Puppy

THE NELSON McCOY POTTERY COMPANY

Factory - Office   Roseville, Ohio

183 - Floral

The Cookie Special caboose, a wishing well, and a wind mill were among cookie jars included in this "hand decorated" display.

1958 Fall Cookie Jar Line

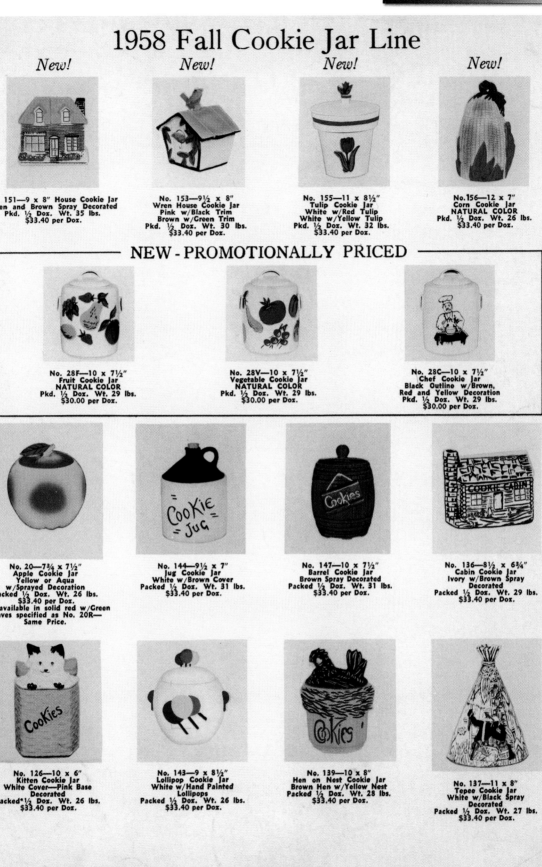

New!

No. 151—9 x 8" House Cookie Jar
Green and Brown Spray Decorated
Pkd. ½ Doz. Wt. 35 lbs.
$33.40 per Doz.

New!

No. 153—9½ x 8"
Wren House Cookie Jar
Pink w/Black Trim
Brown w/Green Trim
Pkd. ½ Doz. Wt. 30 lbs.
$33.40 per Doz.

New!

No. 155—11 x 8½"
Tulip Cookie Jar
White w/Red Tulip
White w/Yellow Tulip
Pkd. ½ Doz. Wt. 32 lbs.
$33.40 per Doz.

New!

No. 156—12 x 7"
Corn Cookie Jar
NATURAL COLOR
Pkd. ½ Doz. Wt. 26 lbs.
$33.40 per Doz.

NEW - PROMOTIONALLY PRICED

No. 28F—10 x 7½"
Fruit Cookie Jar
NATURAL COLOR
Pkd. ½ Doz. Wt. 29 lbs.
$30.00 per Doz.

No. 28V—10 x 7½"
Vegetable Cookie Jar
NATURAL COLOR
Pkd. ½ Doz. Wt. 29 lbs.
$30.00 per Doz.

No. 28C—10 x 7½"
Chef Cookie Jar
Black Outline w/Brown,
Red and Yellow Decoration
Pkd. ½ Doz. Wt. 29 lbs.
$30.00 per Doz.

No. 20—7¾ x 7½"
Apple Cookie Jar
Yellow or Aqua
w/Sprayed Decoration
Packed ½ Doz. Wt. 26 lbs.
$33.40 per Doz.
Also available in solid red w/Green
Leaves specified as No. 20R—
Same Price.

No. 144—9½ x 7"
Jug Cookie Jar
White w/Brown Cover
Packed ½ Doz. Wt. 31 lbs.
$33.40 per Doz.

No. 147—10 x 7½"
Barrel Cookie Jar
Brown Spray Decorated
Packed ½ Doz. Wt. 31 lbs.
$33.40 per Doz.

No. 136—8½ x 6¾"
Cabin Cookie Jar
Ivory w/Brown Spray
Decorated
Packed ½ Doz. Wt. 29 lbs.
$33.40 per Doz.

No. 126—10 x 6"
Kitten Cookie Jar
White Cover—Pink Base
Decorated
Packed ½ Doz. Wt. 26 lbs.
$33.40 per Doz.

No. 143—9 x 8½"
Lollipop Cookie Jar
White w/Hand Painted
Lollipops
Packed ½ Doz. Wt. 26 lbs.
$33.40 per Doz.

No. 139—10 x 8"
Hen on Nest Cookie Jar
Brown Hen w/Yellow Nest
Packed ½ Doz. Wt. 28 lbs.
$33.40 per Doz.

No. 137—11 x 8"
Tepee Cookie Jar
White w/Black Spray
Decorated
Packed ½ Doz. Wt. 27 lbs.
$33.40 per Doz.

House, wren house, tulip, and corn cookie jars were advertised as new in the 1958 fall McCoy catalog.

Ceramic Cookie Jars
HAND DECORATED
May be Assorted—
3 Styles to 6 pack

★ No. 243
Cookie Kettle
8" x 8"

★ No. 171
Kookie Kettle
9 ½" x 8"

★ No. 236—Country Stove
6 ½" x 6 ½" x 10 ½"

★ No. 190—Stove—9" x 9"

No. 244—Aladdin—9" x 7"

No. 213—Early American—7" x 8 ½"

No. 178—Oaken Bucket—9" x 8 ½"

No. 232—Cookie Mug—
9" x 9"

No. 179—Coffee Grinder—
10" x 7"

No. 180—Wishing Well—
9" x 7 ¼"

No. 188—Black Kettle—
8 ½" x 8"

The Nelson McCoy Pottery Company
Area Code 614 697-7331   Roseville, Ohio 43777

Brown was the color of the day in this grouping of ceramic cookie jars.

Hand Crafted Cookie Jars

The Nelson McCoy Pottery Company
Subsidiary of Mount Clemens China Company
Roseville, Ohio 43777

22-7024-16

22-0215-09

22-0159-73

22-0150-73

22-0236-12

Assortment 22-0161-55

22-0235-17

22-0171-04

22-0263-25

22-0262-17

22-0261-25

Assortment 22-0122-55

22-0145-01

22-0156-73

22-0152-08

22-0151-73

22-0148-73

Assortment 22-0162-55

22-0145-01

22-0156-73

22-0846-38

22-0847-38

22-0848-38

Assortment 22-0164-55
Page 2

Assortment 22-0266-55

Assortment 22-0117-55

Along with cookie jars and canister sets in a 1972 McCoy catalog came a retail cookie jar display.

22-0188-45

22-0183-73

47-0195-03

22-0190-71

22-0189-17

22-0182-08

22-0159-73

22-0193-45

Cookie jars advertised in a 1974 McCoy catalog included Grandma, Bobby the Baker, and Freddy.

HAND DECORATED COOKIE JARS

Ass't. 227

No. 253

Ass't. 254

No. 171

No. 236

Ass't. 230

COOKIE JUG

No. 144

No. 7024

No. 255

Ass't. 228

No. 225 Assortment

Ass't. 229

No. 250

No. 213

No. 180

No. 252

No. 178

COOKIES

Wish I Hada Cookie

KOOKIE KETTLE

The Nelson McCoy Pottery Company

Page 2

Area Code 614 697-7331   Roseville, Ohio 43777

More than a dozen of a variety of hand-decorated cookie jars made an appearance in a McCoy catalog.

No. 240—Cookie Jug
9 x 6½"

No. 241—Cookie Log
7½ x 5"

No. 242—Fortune Cookies
9 x 7½"

Ceramic Cookie Jars

HAND DECORATED

See Price List for Assortments

No. 144—Cookie Jug
8½ x 6½"

No. 147—Barrel
8¾ x 6½"

No. 245—Early American Chest
11 x 7"

No. 220—Cookie Pot
10 x 11½"

No. 200—Mediterranean

No. 205—Forbidden Fruit

No. 209—Colonial Fireplace

The Nelson McCoy Pottery Company
Subsidiary of Mount Clemens Pottery Company
Area Code 614 697-7331   Roseville, Ohio 43777

11

A Cookie Log, Fortune Cookies, and Cookie Pot were among this grouping of McCoy cookie jars.

Nelson McCoy

0350-0573
Keebler Tree

COOKIE JARS

A flyer promoted the Keebler Treehouse cookie jar.

Crocks

Crocks and jugs are some of the earliest examples of McCoy wares, and those with salt-glazed surfaces and stenciled lettering are among the most prized.

WF. McCoy 5-gallon crock, salt glaze with stenciled ink lettering: "W.F. McCoy Wholesale Dealer in Stoneware–Zanesville, O.," with impressed "5," late 1800s, 13" tall. **$1,200-$1,400** in mint condition.

WF. McCoy 1 1/2-gallon crock, salt glaze with stenciled ink lettering: "W.F. McCoy Wholesale Dealer in Stoneware–Zanesville, O.," late 1800s, 9 1/4" tall. **$1,000-$1,200**

Three **brown-top miniatures:** plain crock, pickling crock, and jug. Ranging from 3" to 3 3/4" tall. **$175-$225 each**

Three **white crocks** with stenciled shield and "M" mark, in 8-, 12-, and 20-gallon sizes. **$125-150+**

Dinnerware

This section includes tableware pieces used for serving, eating, and drinking. Pieces used to prepare, cook, and store food are found in Kitchenware.

Bunnies baby set (cup not shown), late 1970s, McCoy LCC mark with serial numbers 1221 and 1222, plate 6" diameter. **$35-$40** as shown

Two biscuit jars in glossy cobalt blue and yellow (with cold-paint stripes), 1930s, unmarked. **$75-$90 each**

Left, **biscuit or grease jar** in glossy burgundy, 1950s, unmarked. **$90-$110** Right, **Suburbia creamer** in glossy green, 1960s, McCoy USA mark, 5 1/2" tall. **$45-$55**

Biscuit or cracker jar, glossy maroon, 1930s. **$75-$90**

Three different **1960s candy dishes,** McCoy USA mark. **$25-$35 each**

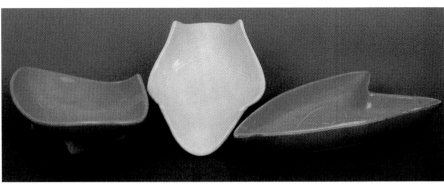

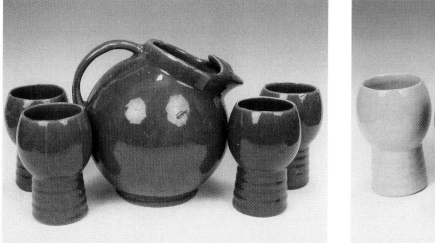

Ball pitcher with ice lip and four goblet-style tumblers in glossy burgundy, 1940s, unmarked; pitcher, 8 1/2" tall. **$50-$60** Tumblers, 5" tall. **$25-$30** each, plus, four goblet-style tumblers in yellow, cobalt blue, aqua, and burgundy.

Ball pitcher in cobalt blue, 1940s, NM mark or unmarked, 6" tall. **$50-$75**

Bean pot, 1950s, McCoy mark, 6" tall. **$65-$75**

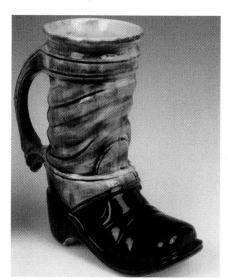

Covered butter dish in glossy green, 1960s, McCoy USA mark. **$30-$40**

Tall Boot stein, 1970s, unmarked, 8" tall. **$25-$30**

Buttermilk pitcher in glossy yellow, late 1920s, unmarked or with shield, usually found in green, sometimes in caramel-tan, 5 1/2" tall. **$60-$70**

Left, **Cabbage salt & pepper shakers** with cork stoppers, 1950s, McCoy USA mark, 4 1/2" tall. **$75-$85/pair** Right, cabbage grease jar, 1950s, McCoy USA, 9" tall. **$125-$150**

A sampling of **Canyon ware,** late 1970s, which included 28 pieces. For a three-piece setting, **$30-$35**

Covered casserole, 1940s, McCoy USA, 6 1/2" diameter. **$55-$65**

Cherries and Leaves teapot, creamer, and sugar in glossy blue (sometimes called plum), mid-1930s, unmarked. Teapot only, **$90-$110** Creamer and sugar, **$90-$110/pair**

Three **Cherries and Leaves teapots** in glossy burgundy, yellow, and aqua, mid-1930s, unmarked. **$90-$110 each**

Cherries and Leaves charger in glossy yellow, mid-1930s, unmarked, 11 1/4" diameter. **$550-$650**

Cherries and Leaves serving bowl, two individual salad bowls, and two cups, all in glossy aqua, mid-1930s, unmarked, all very rare.
Serving bowl, 9" diameter, **$450-$550**
Salad bowls, 5" diameter, **$225-$275 each**
Cups, 2 7/8" tall, **$90-110 each**

Christmas covered sugar, 1970s, **$35-$45**

Cherries and Leaves charger, 11 1/4" diameter, and individual salad bowl, 5" diameter, both in glossy yellow. **Bowl, $225-$275, Charger, $550-$650**

Oil and vinegar cruets with original stand, mismatched stoppers, part of the "Citro-Ramics" line, early 1960s (originally sold for $1.60), McCoy USA mark, ex-Ty Kuhn collection, 9" tall plus stand. **$125-$150/pair**

Cucumber and "Mango" salt & pepper shakers with cork stoppers, 1950s, McCoy USA mark, 5 1/4" tall. **$90-$110/pair**

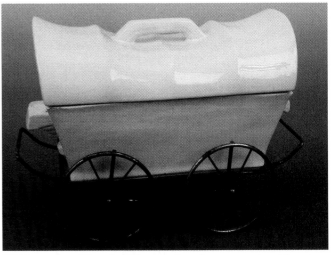

El Rancho Chuck Wagon food warmer, with wire base, 1960s, unmarked, 12" long. **$175-$200**

Two **Bicentennial mugs**, USA mark. **$15+**

Six **Boy Scouts of America mugs** commemorating annual events, some dated (here, 1970s), hundreds of variations with transfer decoration. **$5-$10**

Gorilla mug, late 1970s, McCoy LCC mark, 4 1/2" tall. **$25-$35**

Five variations of the **Smiling Face mugs,** 1970s, McCoy mark, 4" tall. **$15-$20 each**

Smile America mug, 1976. **$18-$22**

Six **sports-theme mugs,** late '80s, unmarked, 4" to 4 1/2" tall. As a set, **$150**, but individual mugs may be valued at **$30.**

Two **Cloverleaf pitchers** with open ice lip, late 1940s, McCoy USA mark, 7" tall. **$45-$55 each**

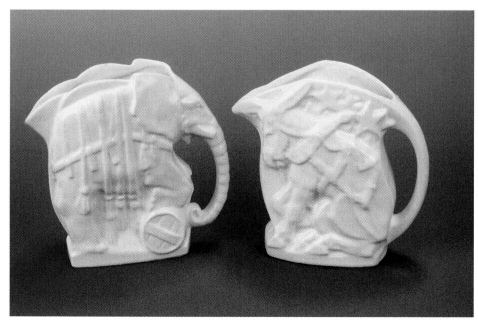

Elephant and Donkey pitchers (also called pitcher vases) in matte white, 1940s, NM USA mark, rare in any color. **$300-$350 each**

Two **Donkey pitchers** (also called pitcher vases) in glossy green and white, 1940s, NM USA mark, rare in any color. **$300-$350 each**

Left, **Donkey pitcher** in glossy aqua, 1940s, NM USA mark. **$300-$350** Right, **Elephant pitcher** in rare burgundy, 1940s, NM USA mark. **$4,000+**

Two **Fish pitchers** (also called pitcher vases), late 1940s, McCoy mark. **$900-$1,000 each**

Grecian teapot, creamer and sugar, 1950s, McCoy USA mark and style number 455, teapot 8" tall with lid. **$125-$150/set**

Three **Hobnail ice-lip jugs,** in yellow, coral, and blue, early 1940s, unmarked. **$150-$175 each**

Two **Hobnail ice-lip pitchers** in glossy burgundy and cobalt blue, 1940s, NM mark and unmarked, 6" tall. **$50-$75 each**

Two **Hobnail ice-lip pitchers** in matte aqua and lavender, 1940s, NM mark or unmarked, 6" tall. **$50-$75 each**

Two **Hobnail ice-lip pitchers** in glossy yellow and lavender, 1940s, NM mark or unmarked, note difference in lip hole sizes, 6" tall. **$50-$75 each**

Ivy teapot, creamer, and sugar in gold trim, 1950s, McCoy USA mark, rarely found in yellow and black. **$275-$325/set**

Two **Parading Ducks pitchers** in glossy brown and burgundy, holds 4 pints, late 1930s, stoneware, unmarked, found in a variety of colors. **$125-$150 each**

Two **Parading Ducks pitchers** in glossy yellow and aqua, holds 4 pints, late 1930s, stoneware, unmarked, found in a variety of colors. **$125-$150 each**

Two **Parrot pitchers** (also called pitcher vases), early 1950s, McCoy USA mark. **$200-$225 each**

Miniature Pig pitcher, not a production piece but marked McCoy, 5 1/2" tall. **$500+**

Miniature Pig pitchers, 1997 from the McCoy Collection, right example in non-production glaze, 6 1/2" tall. **$45-$55 each**

Pine Cone creamer and sugar in gold trim probably done by McCoy, 1950s, McCoy mark. **$70-$80/pair**

Pine Cone teapot, creamer and sugar, 1950s, McCoy mark. **$125-$150/set**

Pitcher and mugs in the Grape pattern in brown and white, late 1920s, stoneware, unmarked, commonly found in green. Pitcher, 8 1/2" tall, **$80-$90**; Mugs, 5" tall, **$20-$25** (Produced at the same time was the Buccaneer pitcher and mugs, almost always in green with shield mark #6 on the mugs, in about the same price range.)

Pitcher and two mugs in green and yellow, 1920s, stoneware, these shapes also found in barrel motif, 9" and 5" tall. Pitcher, **$100-$125**; Mugs, **$30-$35 each** Also, four mugs displayed in a metal rack.

Ring Ware pitcher in glossy green, 1920s, unmarked, 9" tall. **$80-$100**

Ring Ware pitcher and three tumblers in glossy green (note color variations), 1920s, unmarked. Pitcher, 9" tall, **$80-$100**; Tumblers, 4 1/4" tall, **$80-$90 each**

Soup and sandwich set, 1960s, McCoy USA on both, found in other colors. **$25-$35/set**

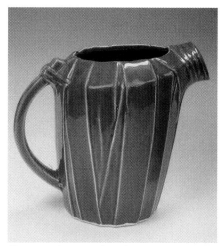

Strap pitcher in glossy burgundy, late 1940s, McCoy mark. **$75-$85**

Two **strap-handle** (also called duck's neck handle) **Berry pitchers** in glossy brown and green, 1930s, unmarked. **$90-$110 each**

Two **Stoneware pitchers** in green (common, also found in yellow) and burgundy, late 1920s, unmarked. Left, 7" tall, **$65-$80**; Right, 7 3/4" tall, **$90-$110**

Left, **W.C. Fields pitcher** (came packaged with decanter), 1970s, 7" tall. **$45-$55** Right, non-production **Grapes-motif pitcher** in matte blue, marked with conjoined "TK" (Ty Kuhn), 7" tall. **$50-$60**

Three **Water Lily pitchers** with Fish handles in tan and white, mid-1930s, unmarked. 7", **$85-$100**; 5 1/2", **$60-$70** (not commonly found in white).

Left, **Water Lily pitcher** with Fish handle in glossy green, mid-1930s, unmarked, 5 1/2" tall. **$60-$70** Right, **Bird and Cherries pitcher,** mid-1930s, unmarked, 5" tall. **$45-$55**

Creations in Ceramics

NEW! OVENPROOF Suburbia Ware!

by The Nelson McCoy Pottery Company

McCoy advertised "New! Ovenproof Suburbia Ware!" in this undated Creations in Ceramics promotion.

Serving
Accessories

Designs by NELSON

attractive ware
for informal serving

McCoy called its Hostess set of serving accessories "attractive ware for informal serving."

Platters, Casseroles & Baking Dishes

KITCHEN ACCESSORIES

28-9370

28-9371

28-0127-62

28-0126-62

28-9375

28-9374

28-0321-01

28-9380-01

28-9381-01

28-0326-01

28-0322-01

28-0320-01

28-0326-01

28-0326-01

The Nelson McCoy Pottery Company
Subsidiary of Mount Clemens China Company
Roseville, Ohio 43777

Page 10

Serving platters for turkey, chicken, and fish, along with some fondue pots, were displayed in a 1973 McCoy catalog.

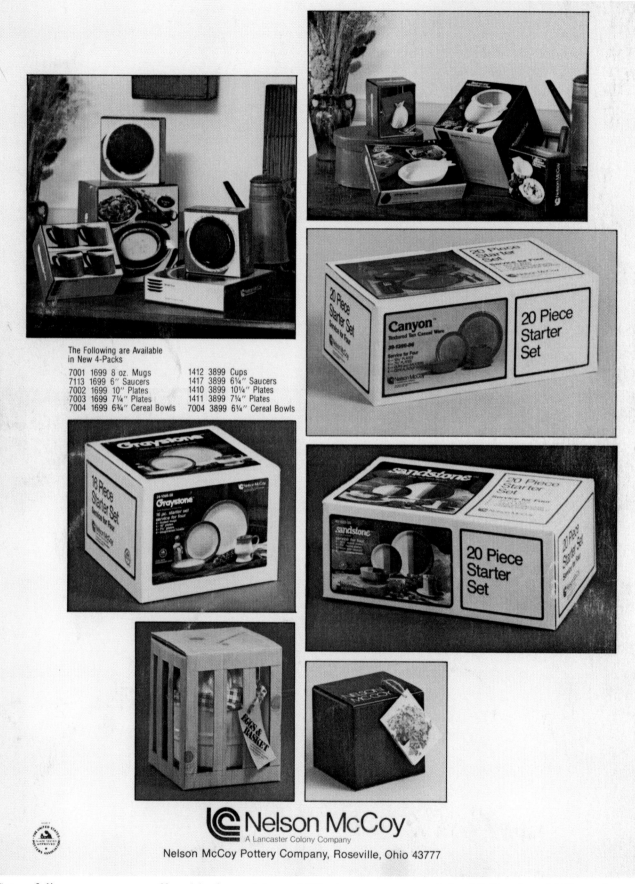

The Following are Available
in New 4-Packs

7001	1699	8 oz. Mugs		1412	3899	Cups
7113	1699	6" Saucers		1417	3899	6¼" Saucers
7002	1699	10" Plates		1410	3899	10¼" Plates
7003	1699	7¼" Plates		1411	3899	7¼" Plates
7004	1699	6¾" Cereal Bowls		7004	3899	6¼" Cereal Bowls

Nelson McCoy
A Lancaster Colony Company

Nelson McCoy Pottery Company, Roseville, Ohio 43777

Sets of dinnerware were offered in four-, 16-, and 20-piece arrangements by McCoy in a 1979 catalog.

Experiments

Experimental pieces often served as tests for new glazes and may have inscribed number and letter codes. Though not common, they can be difficult to value since there is little basis for comparison. Still, collectors prize them as production oddities.

Left, blue and tan glaze on a **baluster vase;** right, part of an **Apple wall pocket** with burgundy glaze; ex-Ty Kuhn collection, with glaze marks. **$60-$70 each**

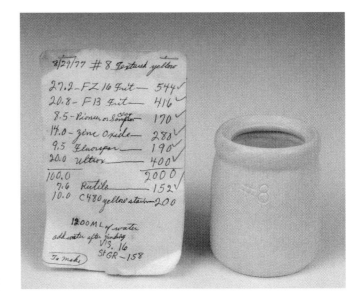

Small jar with textured yellow glaze, inscribed #8, with glaze formula written by Ty Kuhn. **$70-$90**

Two 3" **flower pots** with speckled beige and blue glazes, inscribed on the bottom with glaze numbers, ex-Ty Kuhn collection. **$50-$60 each**

Tyrus Raymond Kuhn - better known as Ty Kuhn - started out painting stoneware jars and eventually became Managing Ceramic Engineer during a 49-year career at the McCoy pottery. His collection of more than 700 pieces of pottery, including many test items and one-of-a-kind examples, was sold at auction in Roseville, Ohio, in 2002.

Bottom of **pitcher flower holder** done in a test glaze with the mark, "X 79," which was a glossy coral. **$150-$200**

Two **mini jugs,** the left marked "#3 bamboo," the right with eagle decal, 5 1/2" tall, ex-Ty Kuhn collection. **$40-$50 each**

Left, **planter** in dark olive glaze, Lancaster Colony, ex-Ty Kuhn collection. **$35-$40** Right, a pair of **chafing dishes** in forest green glaze, ex-Ty Kuhn collection. **$40/pair**

Two **Basket-weave pots and saucers,** 3" and 4", in atypical purple and blue-green glazes, ex-Ty Kuhn collection. **$35-$40 each**

Pitcher, hand-painted by Betty Ford, known for painting apples and roosters on Watt Ware pieces, 6" tall. **$75** This pitcher in factory glaze, **$45**

Shell soap dishes in various trial glazes, with either a tripod foot or three button feet, late 1970s. **$30-$35 each**

Flowerpots have a devoted following among McCoy collectors. While many pots are simple and unadorned utilitarian pieces, the challenge has become finding them in their various sizes and glazes. Many pots are unmarked, but familiarity with designs and glazes helps with attribution.

Butterfly Line pot and saucer in matte aqua and yellow, 1940s, NM USA mark, 6 1/2" diameter. **$75-$85**

Four **Butterfly Line pots and saucers** in matte blue, coral, aqua, and yellow, 1940s, NM USA mark, 3 1/4" diameter. **$55-$65 each** (Note variation in mold crispness; a sharp mold can add to the price.)

Two **Dragonfly pots and saucers** in matte coral and yellow, 1940s, unmarked, 3 1/2" diameter. **$60-$70 each**

Two **Brick pots** in matte aqua, early 1940s, NM USA mark. 7" tall, **$100-$120**; 4 1/4" tall, **$65-$75**

Leaves and Berries flowerpot in matte brown and green, 5 1/2" diameter. **$60-$70**

Two **Leaves and Berries flowerpots** in matte white, unmarked, 4 1/2" and 5" diameter. **$45-$55**

Three **Quilted Rose pots and saucers** in matte white, unmarked 3", 5", and 5 1/2" tall. **$40-$50 each**

Two **Sand Dollar pots and saucers** in matte white, 1940s, unmarked, 4" and 6" tall. **$40-$50 each** (Note difference in mold details: the left is crisp and the right is soft.)

Three **Dragonfly pots**, two with saucers, in matte white, 1940s, unmarked. 3 1/2" tall, **$40-$50**; 4 1/2" tall, **$50-$60**; 5 1/2" tall, **$60-$70**

Bulb planter (also called "the Viking helmet") in glossy white, 1950s, 5" tall. **$50-$60** Right, **pot and saucer** in matte white, 1930s, unmarked, 4" tall. **$25-$30**

Two sizes of the **"Viney" pots,** one with saucer, in matte white, 1930s, unmarked. 9" tall, **$125-$150**; 5" tall, **$70-$80**

Left, **Leafy flowerpot** in glossy ivory glaze, late 1940s, unmarked, 7" tall. **$110-$125**
Right, **Ivy pot** in matte white, 1930s, unmarked, 6" tall. **$50-$60**

Three **Roses on a Wall pots and saucers** in glossy green, 1950s, McCoy mark, also found in pink, white, and yellow. From left, 3 7/8", 5", 4 1/4" tall. **$25-$45 each**

Three **textured pots and saucers** in glossy green, 1950s, McCoy mark. From left, 3", 5", and 4" tall. **$25-$45 each**, with the smallest being the most expensive.

Two **Icicles pots and saucers** in yellow and green, 1950s, McCoy mark, unglazed border is easily soiled and tough to clean, 4 1/2" and 3 7/8" tall. **$25-$30 each**

Pot with test glazes applied, ex-Ty Kuhn collection, 5" tall. **$150-$200.**

Three sizes of **flowerpots** in pale green, 1950s, McCoy USA mark, 7", 6 1/4", and 4 1/4" tall. **$75-$100 each**

Three **Dragonfly pots and saucers** in matte blue (sometimes called "butterfly blue) and aqua, 1940s, unmarked.
6" diameter, **$90-$110**;
5" diameter, **$75-$85**;
3 1/2" diameter, **$60-$70**

Two **pots** in atypical glossy golden glaze. Left, 1930s, McCoy mark, 6" tall. **$35-$45** Right, 1940s, unmarked, 4 1/2" tall. **$25-$35**

Two **Green Thumb pots and saucers**, 1970s, McCoy USA mark with style numbers 0375 and 0373, 6" and 5" tall. **$20-$25 each**

Three **Basket-weave and Leaves pots and saucers** in matte yellow, aqua, and blue, 1940s, NM USA mark, 5 1/2" tall. **$50-$60 each**

Two **Basket-weave and Leaves pots and saucers** in matte blue and yellow, 1940s, NM USA mark, 7 1/2" tall. **$65-$75 each**

Three sizes of **Hobnail pots and saucers** in matte yellow and white, 1940s, NM USA mark. 6" tall, **$90-$110**; 5" tall, **$60-$70**; 3 3/4" tall, **$50-$60**

Two **Hobnail and Leaves pots and saucers** in matte white and blue, 1940s, NM USA mark, 4" and 3 1/2" tall. **$50-$60 each**

Three sizes of **Ribbed pots and saucers** in matte green, green and brown, and white, 1930s, unmarked. 6" tall, **$90-$110**; 5" tall, **$80-$90**; 4" tall, **$60-$70**

Three sizes of **Lily Bud pots and saucers** in matte blue, rose, and yellow, 1940s, NM USA mark.
6" tall, **$65-$75**;
5" tall, **$50-$60**;
3 1/2" tall, **$40-$50**

Four sizes of **Leaf and Flowers pots and saucers** in glossy burgundy, matte green and brown, and matte white, 1930s, stoneware, unmarked.
7" tall, **$125-$150** (less for other matte colors);
6" tall, **$65-$75**;
5" tall, **$50-$60**;
4" tall, **$60-$70**

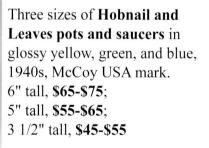

Three sizes of **Hobnail and Leaves pots and saucers** in glossy yellow, green, and blue, 1940s, McCoy USA mark.
6" tall, **$65-$75**;
5" tall, **$55-$65**;
3 1/2" tall, **$45-$55**

Four sizes of **Flat-Leaf pots and saucers** in glossy blue and burgundy, and matte green, 1940s, unmarked.
6 1/2" tall, **$90-$110**;
5 1/2" tall, **$80-$90**;
4" tall, **$65-$75**;
3" tall, **$65-$75**

Three sizes of **Reeded pots and saucers** in matte yellow, coral, and blue, 1940s, NM USA mark.
6" tall, **$65-$75**;
5" tall, **$55-$65**;
4" tall, **$45-$55**

Three **Lotus Leaf pots and saucers** (sometimes saucer is detached) in glossy tan and green, matte brown and green, and glossy green, 1930s, unmarked.
6" tall, **$75-$85**;
4" tall, **$50-$60**

Three sizes of **pots and saucers** in matte white and pink, early 1960s, McCoy USA mark. 6" tall, **$40-$50**; 5" tall, **$35-$40**; 4" tall, **$30-$35**

Lotus Leaf pot and saucer (detached) in brown and green, 1930s, unmarked, 10" tall. **$350-$450**

Two **Basket-weave with Rings pots and saucers** in glossy burgundy and green, 1950s, unmarked. 6" tall, **$75-$85**; 4" tall, **$50-$60**

Large pot and saucer (detached) in glossy yellow, late 1930s, unmarked, 11" tall. **$160-$175**

Pot and saucer (detached) in glossy burgundy, 1940s, unmarked, 9 1/2" tall. **$125-$150**

Two **pots and saucers** (detached) in glossy cobalt blue and green, 1940s, unmarked, 6 1/2" and 5" tall. **$65-$75 each**

Two 4" **pots and saucers** in matte blue and glossy burgundy, early 1940s, unmarked. **$50-$60 each**

Two **Sand Dollar pots and saucers** (sometimes referred to as "NECCO" style, after the round wafer cookie) in glossy green and yellow, 1930s, unmarked. 6" tall, **$55-$65**; 4" tall, **$45-$55**

Four **textured pots and saucers** in glossy pink, green, brown, and yellow, late 1950s, McCoy mark. 6" tall, **$45-$55**; 5" tall, **$35-$40**; 4" tall, **$30-$35**; 3" tall, **$20-$25**

Garden Club pot and saucer in glossy yellow, late 1950s, McCoy USA mark, 8" tall. **$80-$90**

Four assorted **pots** in glossy cobalt blue and burgundy, matte green, and glossy yellow, 3" to 4" tall. **$35-$45 each** (Cobalt blue pot at left is attributed to McCoy.)

Garden Club pot in glossy turquoise, late 1950s, McCoy USA mark, 9" tall. **$80-$90**

Two **Garden Club pots and saucers** in matte green, late 1950s, McCoy USA mark. 3 1/2" tall, **$45-$55**, 5 1/2" tall, **$55-$65**;

Garden Club pot and saucer in glossy green, late 1950s, McCoy USA mark, 7 1/4" tall. **$65-$75**

Two **Hobnail pots and saucers** with stylized Greek key bands in glossy pink and yellow, 1940s, McCoy mark, 5" and 4" tall. **$30-$40 each**

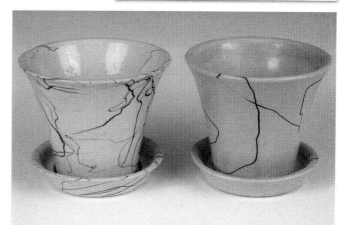

Two **"Squiggle" pots and saucers** in glossy yellow and matte pink, 1960s, McCoy USA mark, 5 1/2" tall. **$50-$60**

Two **Quilted pots and saucers** in glossy green and yellow, 1950s, McCoy USA mark, 5" tall and 4" tall. **$30-$35 each**

Two **Quilted Roses pots and saucers** in glossy pink and brown, 1950s, McCoy USA mark, 5" tall. **$65-$75 each**

Two **Daisy pots and saucers,** 1950s, McCoy USA mark. 6 1/2" tall, **$65-$75**. 4" tall, **$45-$55**

Two **matte brown pots,** one with saucer, late 1970s, McCoy LCC mark, 4 1/2" and 5" tall. **$40-$50 each**

Three assorted **pots and saucers** in glossy green and yellow, and matte brown and green, 1930s, unmarked, 3" to 4" tall. **$40-$60 each** (Green pot is attributed to McCoy.)

Two **Swirl pots and saucers** in semi-gloss green, 1950s, McCoy USA mark, 6" and 4" **$25-$35 each**

Two **Speckled pots and saucers** in glossy turquoise and pink, 1950s, McCoy USA mark, 6" and 4" tall. **$25-$35 each**

Two **Fish-scale pots and saucers** in glossy blue and yellow, 1940s, NM USA mark. 7" tall. **$55-$65**; 4" tall, **$40-$45**

Two **Brocade Line pots and saucers** in pink and black and pink and green, 1950s, McCoy USA mark, 6" tall. **$50-$60 each**

Three **Reeded pots and saucers** in semi-gloss pink, yellow, and green, 1940s, NM USA mark.
6" tall, **$55-$65;**
5" tall, **$45-$55**;
4" tall, **$35-$40**

Three **pots and saucers**, McCoy USA marks. Left and right, 3" tall, **$20-$30 each**; center, **Icicles** in blue, 6 1/2" tall. **$40-$50**

Pot in test glaze, ex-Ty Kuhn collection. **$100+**

Two **pots and saucers**. Left, glossy turquoise, 1930s, unmarked, 6" tall. **$65-$75** Right, **Ring Ware** in glossy green, 1930s, unmarked, 5 1/2" tall. **$75-$85**

Butterfly line pot, 1940s, NM USA mark, 4 1/2" in tall. **$45-$55**

The Tiara Line

31-0693-84

31-0692-84

50-0546-00

50-0500-06

The Nelson McCoy Pottery Company
Subsidiary of Mount Clemens Pottery Company
Area Code 614 697-7331   Roseville, Ohio 43777

31-0670-01

31-0671-01

31-0672-01

31-3014-01

31-0612

31-3009-01

31-3008-01

31-0634
31-0635
31-0636
31-0637

31-0631
31-0632
31-0633

31-0667

31-0627

31-0628
31-0629

31-1488-01
31-1480-01

31-0613

Page 19

McCoy's Tiara Line featured a variety of flowerpots and planters in many shapes and sizes, including a car, a frog, and a deer.

38-0032-01

38-0035-01

38-0033-01

Scandia Line

38-0031-01

38-0034-01

38-0030-01

The Nelson McCoy Pottery Company
Subsidiary of Mount Clemens China Company
Roseville, Ohio 43777

38-0037-01

38-0036-01

38-0677-01

38-0620-01

Page 24

Photography and Lithography by Pappas Brothers, Parkersburg, W.Va.

A basic pattern was carried through in several sizes and colors of flowerpots in a 1972 catalog.

Hand decorated modernistic designs. Simple lines that accent the floral arrangement. Priced for volume sales at a profit.

900 - 6"
904 - 6"
905 - 7"
902 - 8½"
901 - 9¼"
907 - 7½"
908 - 12"
906 - 9¼"
903 - 12"

THE NELSON McCOY POTTERY COMPANY
Factory - Office   Roseville, Ohio

The Harmony line of flowerpots and vases featured "hand decorated modernistic designs," according to McCoy.

Green Thumb

33-0541-46

50-0551-06

50-0552-06

44-0393-01

44-0389-01

44-0392-01

44-0388-01

44-0376-01

44-0377-01

44-0378-01

31-3010-01

50-0532-13

44-0386-17

27

Among McCoy's largest lines of flowerpots was the Green Thumb line in many shapes and sizes.

Jardinières and Pedestal

From the earliest blended and matte glazes made just after the turn of the 19th century to the late incarnations of the 1970s, "jards and peds" (as collectors call them) are a challenging area for treasure hunters trying to match tops and bottoms. Many are unmarked.

Basket-Weave jardinière in matte yellow, 6 3/4" tall. **$70-$80**

Jardinière and pedestal in glossy turquoise and cobalt blue drip glaze, circa 1910, 41" tall overall, unmarked. **$1,500-$2,000**

Basket-Weave jardinière in matte aqua, 7 1/2" diameter. **$80-$100**

Basket-Weave jardinière and pedestal in matte white, jardinière 7 1/2" diameter, pedestal (NM USA mark) 13" tall. **$300-$350/pair**

Basket-Weave jardinière in matte brown and green, 1930s, unmarked, 9" tall. **$350-$450**

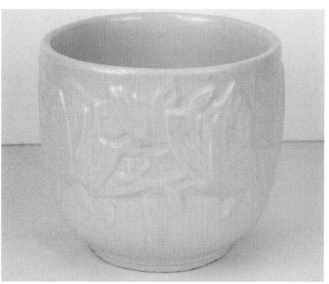

Butterfly jardinière, matte yellow, 7" tall, NM mark. **$125-$150**

Two **Butterfly jardinières** in matte white, both NM mark.
3 1/2" diameter, **$30-$40**;
7 1/2" diameter, **$125-$150**

Holly jardinière in matte brown and green, 5" tall. **$40-$50 Leaves and Berries flowerpot** with saucer in matte brown and green, 4 1/2" tall. **$40-$50**

Three **Holly jardinières** in matte green. 5", **$40-$50**; 7 1/2", **$80-$90**; 4" diameter, **$30-$40**

Left and right, two 4" **Leaves and Berries jardinières** in matte green showing variations in color and mold crispness, 1930s, unmarked. **$35-$45**
A 5" **Holly jardinière** in matte green, 1930s, unmarked. **$45-$55**

Holly jardinière and pedestal in matte green, unmarked, jardinière 7 1/2" diameter, pedestal 13" tall. **$300-$350/pair**

Leaves and Berries jardinière and pedestal in matte brown and green, jardinière 7 1/2" diameter, pedestal 6 3/4" tall. **$225-$275/ pair**

Leaves and Berries jardinière and pedestal in matte green, jardinière 8 1/2" diameter, pedestal 12 1/2" tall. **$300-$400/ pair**

Leaves and Berries jardinière and pedestal in matte green, jardinière 7 1/2" diameter, pedestal 6 1/2" tall. **$225-$275/ pair**

Leaves and Berries jardinière and pedestal in matte white, jardinière 8 1/2" diameter, pedestal 12 3/4" tall. **$250-$300**

Leaves and Berries jardinière in matte brown and green, 1930s, unmarked, 4" diameter. **$50-$60**

Lily Bud jardinière, 1940s, NM USA mark, 7 1/2" diameter. **$55-$65**

Oak Leaves and Acorns jardinière in matte green, 5" diameter, and **Holly jardinière** in matte green, 4" diameter. **$40-$50 each**

Oak Leaves and Acorns jardinière in matte green, late 1920s, unmarked, 6 3/4" tall. **$70-$80**

Quilted jardinière in matte white, 9" diameter. **$90-$100** Oak Leaves and Acorns jardinière in matte white, 7 1/2" diameter. **$60-$70**

Quilted jardinière and pedestal in matte white, jardinière 7 1/2" diameter, pedestal (NM USA mark) 13" tall. **$250-$300**

Sand Butterfly jardinière, matte white, 7" tall. **$60-$70**

Sand Butterfly jardinières in brown and green. 8", **$80-$90**; 5" diameter, **$40-$50**

Swallows jardinière in matte green, 1940s, unmarked, 5" tall. **$40-$50**

Swallows jardinières in matte white, 1940s, unmarked. 7 1/2" diameter, **$90-$110**; 4" diameter, **$50-$60**

Swallows jardinière in matte green, 1940s, unmarked, 7 1/2" diameter. **$80-$90**

Two **Oak Leaves and Acorns jardinières** in matte white, late 1920s, unmarked. 6 1/2" tall, **$70-$80**; 4 1/4" tall, **$45-$55**

Two **Leaves and Berries straight-side jardinières** in matte white, 1930s, unmarked. 6 1/2" tall, **$90-$110**; 4 1/4" tall, **$50-$60**

Holly jardinière in matte white, 1930s, unmarked, 9" tall. **$175-$225**

Two **Swallows jardinières** in cobalt blue and matte white, 1940s, unmarked, 7" tall, **$90-$110**, with cobalt being slightly higher.

Left, **Basket-weave jardinière** in matte white, 1930s, NM mark or unmarked, 7 1/2" tall. Right, **Morning Glory jardinière** in matte white, late 1920s, unmarked, 6 1/2" tall. **$70-$80 each**

Leaves and Berries jardinière and pedestal in matte white, 1930s, no mark; jardinière, 7 1/2" tall; pedestal, 13" tall. **$350-$450/pair** (In glossy blended glazes, add $100.)

Sand Butterfly jardinière and pedestal in matte white, 1930s, unmarked; jardinière, 9" tall; pedestal, 13 1/4" tall. **$300-$350/pair**

Ivy jardinière in brown and green, early 1950s, unmarked, also found in a brighter glossy tan and green with matching pedestal, 8" tall. **$350-$450**

Left, **Vertical ribbed jardinière**, glossy aqua glaze, 1930s, shield mark, 6 1/2" tall. **$45-$60**
Right, **Leaves and Berries footed vase** in matte green, stoneware, also found in other matte colors and cobalt blue, 1930s, unmarked, 7" tall. **$75-$100**

Jardinière in glossy green, 1950s, unmarked, 8" tall. **$70-$90**

Smallest Swallows jardinière in matte blue, 1940s, unmarked, 4" tall. **$55-$65**

Two **hook jardinières** in glossy burgundy, 1940s, NM mark or unmarked. 7 1/2", **$50-$60**; 4 1/2" diameter, **$30-$40**

Fish in Net jardinière in rare gray-green, late 1950s, McCoy mark, also found in brown, 7 1/2" tall. **$250-$300**

Two **jardinières** with applied leaves and berries, late 1940s, McCoy USA mark, 7 1/2" tall. **$200-$250 each**

Jardinière in matte aqua, stoneware, in floral pattern, 1930s, unmarked, 7 1/2" tall. **$70-$80**

Two **hook jardinières** in glossy aqua, 1940s, NM mark or unmarked. 7 1/2" diameter, **$50-$60**. 3 3/4" diameter, **$25-$30**

Three sizes of **Hobnail jardinières** in matte aqua, 1940s, NM USA mark, found in other matte colors.
3" tall, **$35-$40**;
4" tall, **$45-$50**;
6 1/2" tall, **$75-$85**

Two **Grecian jardinières** (5 1/2" and 4 1/2" tall), 1950s, McCoy USA mark and style number 443 on jardinières. **$50-$60 each**

Butterfly Line pieces in matte aqua. Left, smallest jardinière, 1940s, NM USA mark, 3 1/4" diameter. **$45-$50**
Right, Square-top jardinière, USA mark, 3 3/4" square. **$55-$65**

Sand Butterfly jardinière
in matte aqua (rare color),
stoneware, 1930s, unmarked,
usually found white or in brown
and green, 4" tall. **$55-$65**

Jardinière in matte white,
1950s, McCoy USA mark,
7" tall. **$50-$60**

Hook jardinière in matte white,
1940s, 3" tall. **$25-$35**

Two **Butterfly Line pieces** in matte
aqua and yellow. Left, square-top
footed jardinière, 1940s, USA mark,
5 1/4" square. **$110-$125**
Right, square-top footed jardinière,
1940s, USA mark, 3 3/4" square.
$55-$65

Jardinieres   Jardinieres & Peds
Pet Feeders

No. 421C—6" Sq. Jardiniere
Amethyst inside—Pink outside
Mustard inside—Brown outside
Packed 1 Doz. Wt. 23 lbs.
$14.40 per Dozen

No. 412—7½" Jardiniere
Brown Spray or Green Spray
Packed 1 Doz. Wt. 42 lbs.
$17.60 per Dozen

No. 47—7½" Jardiniere
Yellow or White
Packed 1 Doz. Wt. 52 lbs.
$14.40 per Dozen

No. 58 Jardiniere
Sizes 4½"-5½"-6½"-7½"-
8½"-9½"-10½"
Green, White, Yellow

4½"—$ 6.70 per Doz.	3 Doz. 37 lbs.
5½"—$ 8.40 per Doz.	2 Doz. 40 lbs.
6½"—$10.20 per Doz.	1½ Doz. 42 lbs.
7½"—$14.40 per Doz.	1½ Doz. 42 lbs.
8½"—$20.00 per Doz.	2/3 Doz. 37 lbs.
9½"—$24.60 per Doz.	2/3 Doz. 50 lbs.
10½"—$32.00 per Doz.	1/3 Doz. 36 lbs.

No. 48—Jardinieres
Sizes 8½"-10½"
Green or White
8½"—$20.00 per Doz. 2/3 Doz. 47 lbs.
10½"—$32.00 per Doz. 1/3 Doz. 40 lbs.

No. 48—Jar and Ped.
Green and White
8½" Jard. and 12½" Pedestal
1 only—18 lbs.
$5.30 each

No. 3—10" Porch Jar
White or Green
Packed 1/3 Doz. Wt. 57 lbs.
Available with or without
Drainage—please specify
$4.00 each

The 1958 McCoy catalog featured a variety of jardinières, as well as a porch jar.

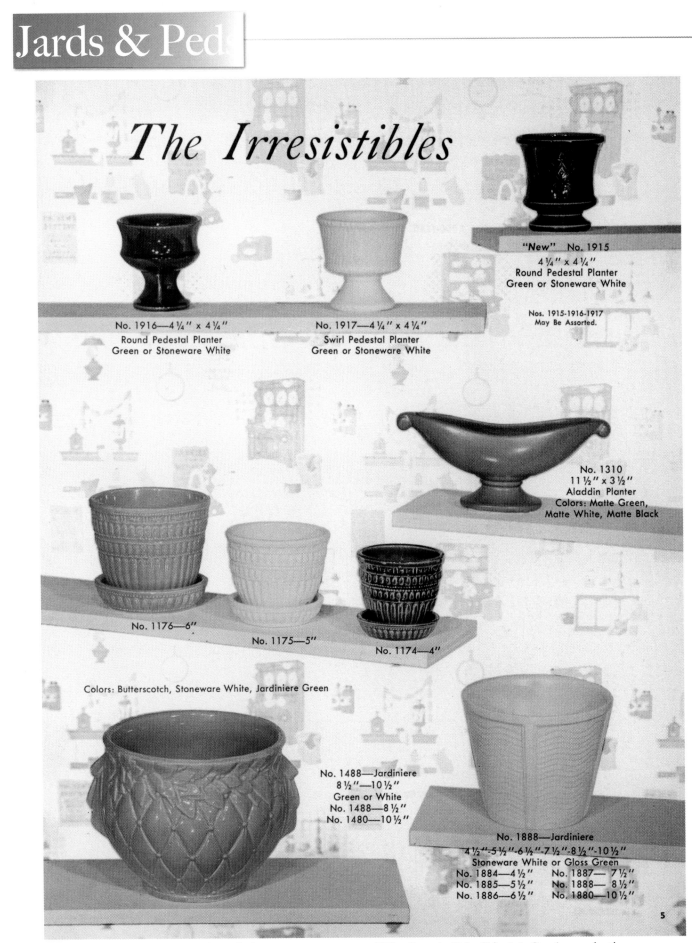

The Irresistibles

"New" No. 1915
4 ¼" x 4 ¼"
Round Pedestal Planter
Green or Stoneware White

Nos. 1915-1916-1917
May Be Assorted.

No. 1916—4 ¼" x 4 ¼"
Round Pedestal Planter
Green or Stoneware White

No. 1917—4 ¼" x 4 ¼"
Swirl Pedestal Planter
Green or Stoneware White

No. 1310
11 ½" x 3 ½"
Aladdin Planter
Colors: Matte Green,
Matte White, Matte Black

No. 1176—6"

No. 1175—5"

No. 1174—4"

Colors: Butterscotch, Stoneware White, Jardiniere Green

No. 1488—Jardiniere
8 ½"—10 ½"
Green or White
No. 1488—8 ½"
No. 1480—10 ½"

No. 1888—Jardiniere
4 ½"-5 ½"-6 ½"-7 ½"-8 ½"-10 ½"
Stoneware White or Gloss Green
No. 1884—4 ½"   No. 1887— 7 ½"
No. 1885—5 ½"   No. 1888— 8 ½"
No. 1886—6 ½"   No. 1880—10 ½"

5

Jardinières and several styles of planters were among "The Irresistibles" in McCoy's marketing.

Jars

This section includes oil jars, porch jars (basically used as big planters), and sand jars (once common in hotel lobbies as receptacles for cigars and cigarettes). Some of the larger stoneware pieces were first made in the 1920s and '30s, but these same designs can still be found on McCoy catalog pages from the 1950s.

Low Sand Butterfly porch jar in matte white, 1930s, unmarked, 11" tall. **$150-$200**

Cherries sand jar in matte white, 1930s, unmarked, 14" by 10". **$350-$450**

Oil jar in glossy aqua, late 1930s, NM mark, 12" tall. **$150-$200**

Porch jar with rings and grape motif in matte white, 1940s, NM mark, 9 1/4" tall. **$175-$225** (in brown and green, **$300-$400**)

Porch jar with tab handles in matte white, 1930s, unmarked, heights can vary from 17 3/8" to 18". No established value in matte white; in brown and green, **$500-$600**

Sand Butterfly porch jar in matte white, 1930s, unmarked, heights can vary from 19 1/2" to just over 20". No established value in matte white; in brown and green, **$550-$650**

Porch jar in matte aqua, with dense Leaves and Berries pattern and double ring handles, 1930s, unmarked, one of only three known, 11 1/2" tall. **$3,500-$4,500**

Oil jar with hand-painted floral decoration by Betty Ford, 1940s, NM mark, 12" tall, with rim chip. If perfect, **$150-$200**

Porch jar with grapes motif in matte aqua, late 1930s, stoneware, NM USA mark, 9 1/2" tall. **$250-$300**

Kitchenware

This section includes pieces used to prepare, cook, and store food. Tableware pieces used for serving, eating, and drinking are found in Dinnerware.

Two sizes of the **batter bowl with spoon rest** in glossy green, late 1920s, shield mark #3, diameters without spouts and handles. 7 1/2", **$175-$225**; 9 1/2", **$275-$325**

Cook-Serve Ware covered casserole and stickhandle creamer, late 1940s, McCoy mark. Casserole, **$35-$40**; Creamer, **$10-$15**

Mixing bowl in the Wave or Sunrise pattern, size No. 7, from a set of six ranging in size from 5" to 11" diameter, 1920s, square bottom, also found in yellow and burgundy; and three 5" mixing bowls in green, yellow, and burgundy. Complete set, about **$1,200**; Individual sizes range from **$175-$250 each**

Two **Ring ware covered vessels** (casseroles?) in glossy green, note different sized knobs, 1920s, shield mark "M"; 3 5/8" and 4" tall not including lids. **$175-$200 each**

Two **square-bottom Ring ware mixing bowls** in green and yellow, 1930s, shield mark with size inside (8" and 9", though they may actually be up to a half inch larger in diameter), also a pattern number (2, indicating the ring pattern). **$150-$175 each**

Three **Raspberries and Leaves mixing bowls** in teal, light burgundy, and blue, 1930s, unmarked, 9" diameter (there may be other sizes). **$200-$225 each**

Raspberries and Leaves mixing bowl in glossy white, 1930s, unmarked, 9" diameter. **$200-$225**

Four **mixing bowls** in the Feather pattern in ivory, yellow, green, and burgundy, 1940s, McCoy mark, 6", 7", and 8" diameter. **$35-$75**

Various sizes of **mixing bowls** with tiny berries in the outer rim and fluted bodies, 1930s, unmarked, sizes include 4", 6", 7", 8", priced in ascending sizes. **$35-$100**

Two **mixing bowls** in glossy pink, 1950s, McCoy USA Oven Proof mark, 5" and 6" diameter. **$35-$45 each** Also found in other sizes.

Five sizes of **Stone Craft mixing bowls** (called pink and blue) ranging in diameter from 7" to 14" (also a 5" size), mid-1970s, McCoy LCC mark. **$225-$250** for complete set

Penguin spoon rest, 1950s, 7" x 5 1/2", **$125-$175**

Two **Islander Line creamers** in yellow and white, early 1980s. **$50-$60 each**

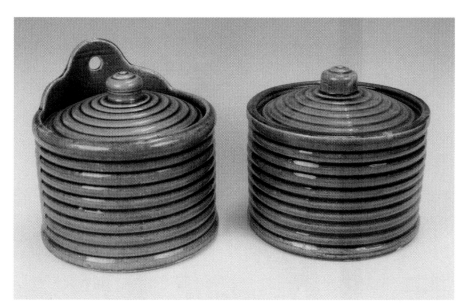

Ring ware hanging salt box and covered jar (cheese or butter), both in glossy green, 1920s, shield mark "M." Salt box, 6" tall, **$250-$300**; Covered jar, 5" tall, **$175-$200**

Ring ware covered butter or cheese crock, 1920s, shield mark "M," **$90-$110**

Wood & White

C58W

BC53W

C57W

SC51W

CC54W

SP52W

CH50W

C55W

S36W

McCoy Limited
26 North Third Street, Zanesville, OH 43701
614/453-6048 or 453-0654

The Wood & White line included a breadboard, condiment set, casserole, bowls, a coffee carafe, and salt & pepper shakers.

Real McCoy Cookware

28-7536-15 Set

28-7532-15

28-7531-15

28-1001-11

28-1003-11

28-1002-11

28-1012-00 Book

28-1010-00 Set

28-0126-77

28-0125-77

Page 9

A set of Real McCoy Cookware in a 1975 catalog included several sizes of cooking pots and casseroles.

Fall 1958 Oven Proof Kitchenware Items
New Flecked Colors ... Turquoise, Yellow Pink

No. 15-FP—Mixing Bowls
Sizes 5", 6", 7", 8"
Turquoise, Yellow, Pink Flecked
Finish
5"—$3.90 per Doz. 3 Doz. 33 lbs.
6"—$5.60 per Doz. 3 Doz. 48 lbs.
7"—$7.50 per Doz. 2 Doz. 44 lbs.
8"—$10.40 per Doz. 1½ Doz. 46 lbs.
3 Pc. Set—6-7-8"
2/3 Doz. Wt. 48 lbs.
4 Pc. Set—5-6-7-8"
2/3 Doz. Wt. 54 lbs.
3 Pc. 6-7-8"—$23.80 per Doz. SETS
4 Pc. 5-6-7-8"—$27.60 per Doz. SETS

No. CM1-F-8 oz. Coffee Mug
Turquoise, Yellow, Pink
Flecked Finish
Pkd. 4 Doz. Wt. 42 lbs.)
$7.20 per Doz.

No. 141-F—48 oz. Pitcher
Turquoise, Yellow, Pink
Flecked Finish
Pkd. 1 Doz. Wt. 32 lbs.
$15.60 per Doz.

No. 105-F—36 oz. Tea Pot
Turquoise, Yellow, Pink
Flecked Finish
Pkd. 1 Doz. Wt. 27 lbs.
$16.00 per Doz.

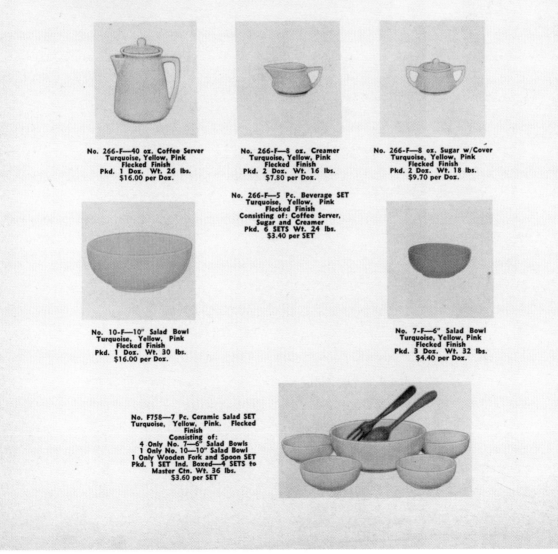

No. 266-F—40 oz. Coffee Server
Turquoise, Yellow, Pink
Flecked Finish
Pkd. 1 Doz. Wt. 26 lbs.
$16.00 per Doz.

No. 266-F—8 oz. Creamer
Turquoise, Yellow, Pink
Flecked Finish
Pkd. 2 Doz. Wt. 16 lbs.
$7.80 per Doz.

No. 266-F—8 oz. Sugar w/Cover
Turquoise, Yellow, Pink
Flecked Finish
Pkd. 2 Doz. Wt. 18 lbs.
$9.70 per Doz.

No. 266-F—5 Pc. Beverage SET
Turquoise, Yellow, Pink
Flecked Finish
Consisting of: Coffee Server,
Sugar and Creamer
Pkd. 6 SETS Wt. 24 lbs.
$3.40 per SET

No. 10-F—10" Salad Bowl
Turquoise, Yellow, Pink
Flecked Finish
Pkd. 1 Doz. Wt. 30 lbs.
$16.00 per Doz.

No. 7-F—6" Salad Bowl
Turquoise, Yellow, Pink
Flecked Finish
Pkd. 3 Doz. Wt. 32 lbs.
$4.40 per Doz.

No. F758—7 Pc. Ceramic Salad SET
Turquoise, Yellow, Pink. Flecked
Finish
Consisting of:
4 Only No. 7—6" Salad Bowls
1 Only No. 10—10" Salad Bowl
1 Only Wooden Fork and Spoon SET
Pkd. 1 SET Ind. Boxed—4 SETS to
Master Ctn. Wt. 36 lbs.
$3.60 per SET

Mixing bowls, a salad set, and a coffee server were among items in the 1958 Oven Proof Kitchenware line in turquoise, yellow, and pink.

Lazy Suzans

No. 900—12"
Chartreuse & Green

No. 900—950
Gift Box

No. 950—12"
Yellow & Birchwood

No. 901—12"
Green & White
Chestnut & Chartreuse

No. 9051—12"
Robin Egg Blue, White
& Oatmeal

No. 910—905
Gift Box

The Nelson McCoy Pottery Company
Area Code 614 697-7331   Roseville, Ohio 43777

8

McCoy highlighted four styles and colors of Lazy Suzans in this promotion.

Durable Ceramic Mixing Bowls

In Gay Colors

No. 871—8" Bowl
Brown

No. 771—7" Bowl
Cranberry

No. 671—6" Bowl
Blue

No. 32—Bowl Set—8", 10", 12"
Pink Fleck, Turquoise & Yellow
Available in Open Stock
As Per Price List.

No. 678—Bowl Set—6", 7", 8"

No. 70—Bean Pot
Brown & Yellow Drip

No. 70—Bean Pot
Brown & Green Drip

No. 51—1½ Gal. Jug

No. 52—1 Gal. Jug
Antique Eagle Jugs
Simulated Salt Glaze Treatment

No. 53—1 Pint Jug

No. 60—1 Gal. Jug
Brown & Gray Specked

The Nelson McCoy Pottery Company
Area Code 614 697-7331   Roseville, Ohio 43777

Several "durable ceramic mixing bowls in gay colors" were featured by McCoy, along with several jugs.

KITCHEN ACCESSORIES

No. 53

No. 52

No. 363

No. 364

No. 365

No. 118-12½"
119-14"

No. 106-6"
108-8"
110-10"
112-12"
114-14"

The Nelson McCoy Pottery Company
Subsidiary of Mount Clemens Pottery Company
Area Code 614 697-7331   Roseville, Ohio 43777

No. 137

No. 138

Page 10

Cups and saucers, pitchers, and mixing bowls were among this grouping of McCoy kitchenware.

CANISTERS
Large Canister will hold 5 lb. Flour, Medium size will hold 5 lb. Sugar, Small sizes will hold 1 lb. Coffee or Tea.

The eating area just in front of a walk-in pantry at the Jagger House.

39-1394-86

40-1531-55

22-0200-08

30-0134-37

28-0223-73

22-0225-08

22-0214-24

24-1090-58

29-7080-16

19

Canister sets in several styles were featured in a 1978 McCoy catalog.

Lamps

Many McCoy lamp bases are unmarked, so comparing glazes can be a clue to their origin. Look for oddities, like vase forms converted to lamps, and for figural bases with atypical glazes.

"Anniversary" or Sunflower lamp base in glossy white, 1930s, unmarked, 8 1/2" tall. **$50-$60**

Cowboy Boots lamp, 1950s, McCoy USA mark, with replacement shade, boots only 7" tall. **$75-$100**

Lamp base in glossy streaked blue onyx glaze, sometimes found in matte glazes, with leafy borders and twig handles, 1940s, unmarked, 9" tall. **$300-$350**

Left, **Stoneware lamp** in matte green, 1940s, 8 1/2" tall. **$350-$450** Right, **Fisherman or Whaling Man lamp base,** 1950s, 16 1/4" tall (reproductions are slightly smaller). **$250-$300** More with original wiring and hardware.

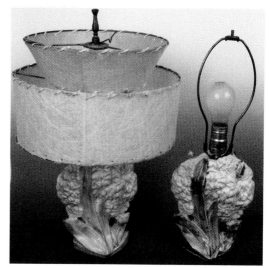

Two **Hyacinth lamps,** made at the McCoy factory but not production pieces, early 1950s, McCoy mark, 8 1/2" tall (pottery only). **$1,800-$2,000 each** (The Hyacinth vases in these colors typically are valued at about **$150-$225**.)

Two white **Stoneware lamps,** early 1940s, unmarked; left, Lily Bud pattern; right, Leaves and Berries; each 5 1/2" tall. **$600-$700 each**

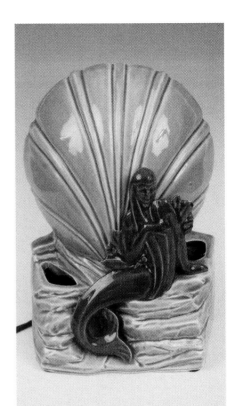

Mermaid TV lamp in gray and burgundy, 1950s, unmarked, also found in black and chartreuse, 9 1/2" tall. **$200-$250**

Fireplace TV lamp/ planter, 1950s, unmarked, also found in chartreuse and black, and with screen behind logs, 9" tall. **$90-$110**

Two **Sunflower lamps**, one in blue-gray, one in burgundy, 1950s, also found in chartreuse, yellow, McCoy USA mark, 9" tall. **$70-$90 each**

Arcature lamp with textured surface, 1950s, McCoy USA mark, base 9" tall. **$110-$125**

Loy-Nel-Art

The J.W. McCoy Pottery Co. began producing Loy-Nel-Art wares in 1905. The line's distinctive title came from the names of James McCoy's three sons, Lloyd, Nelson, and Arthur. Like other "standard" glazed pieces produced at this time by several Ohio potteries, Loy-Nel-Art has a glossy finish on a dark brown-black body, but Loy-Nel-Art featured a splash of green color on the front, and a burnt-orange splash on the back.

Three **Loy-Nel-Art vases** in different shapes, all unmarked. 8", **$175-$225;** 11 1/2" and 12" tall, **$225-$275**

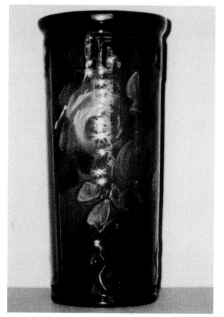

Loy-Nel-Art Greek Key vase with roses, marked Loy-Nel-Art McCoy, 10" tall. **$275-$325**

Loy-Nel-Art vase, marked Loy-Nel-Art McCoy, 10 1/2" tall. **$375-$425**

Loy-Nel-Art vase, unmarked, 7" tall. **$175-$225**

Loy-Nel-Art jardinière, unmarked, 10" tall. **$275-$325**

Two **Loy-Nel-Art vases,** one with pansies and one with cherries, both marked Loy-Nel-Art McCoy, 6 1/2" tall. **$200-$275 each**

Loy-Nel-Art low footed bowl, marked "205-8," 4" by 8 1/2". **$175-$225**

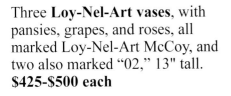

Three **Loy-Nel-Art vases**, with pansies, grapes, and roses, all marked Loy-Nel-Art McCoy, and two also marked "02," 13" tall. **$425-$500 each**

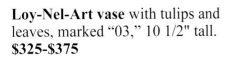

Loy-Nel-Art vase with tulips and leaves, marked "03," 10 1/2" tall. **$325-$375**

Two **Loy-Nel-Art vases** with berries and flowers, both marked "03," 10 1/2" tall. **$325-$375 each**

Loy-Nel-Art jar with cigar decoration, unmarked, 4" by 4". **$250-$300**

Two **Loy-Nel-Art footed jardinières,** one with cherries, one with flowers, both marked Loy-Nel-Art McCoy, 5" by 5 1/2". **$200-$275 each**

Three **Loy-Nel-Art footed jardinières** with floral decoration, all marked Loy-Nel-Art McCoy, 4 1/2" tall. **$175-$250 each**

Loy-Nel-Art pitcher, unmarked, 5 1/2" tall. **$200-$250**

Loy-Nel-Art vase with grapes, unmarked, 12 1/2" tall. **$475-$550**

Loy-Nel-Art umbrella stand, marked Loy-Nel-Art McCoy, 21 1/2" tall. **$950-$1,100**

Non-production **Loy-Nel-Art footed jardinière,** unmarked, 11" by 12" **$750-$825**

Loy-Nel-Art vase with roses, marked Loy-Nel-Art McCoy, 15" tall. **$675-$750**

Two **Loy-Nel-Art footed jardinières** with flowers, marked Loy-Nel-Art McCoy, 8" and 7" tall. **$325-$400 each**

Loy-Nel-Art cuspidor with pansies, marked "206," 8" tall. **$200-$250**

Loy-Nel-Art vase with flowers on the front and raised Indian motif on reverse, unmarked, 12" tall. **$525-$575 each**

Loy-Nel-Art jardinière and pedestal, unmarked; jardinière, 10" tall; pedestal, 18" tall. **$675-$750/pair**

Loy-Nel-Art jardinière and pedestal, unmarked; jardinière, 8" tall; pedestal, 18" tall. **$675 to $750/pair**

Loy-Nel-Art jardinière and pedestal; jardinière, marked Loy-Nel-Art McCoy 205, 9 1/2" tall; pedestal, marked 2050, 16 1/2" tall. **$1,200-$1,400/pair**

Miscellaneous

This section includes ashtrays, bookends, console bowls, boxes, ornaments, and other accessories, and some rare non-production pieces.

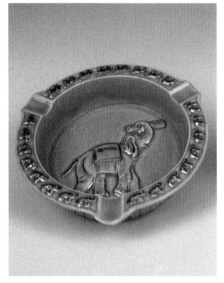

Republican ashtray in gold trim, 1960s, inscribed on bottom, "Designed by Paul Genter," also found in other colors with raised outline of Ohio, 6" diameter, **$45-$50**

Flower form bookends/planters, 1950s, McCoy USA mark, also found in green and yellow, cream and green; 6" tall. **$150-$175/pair**

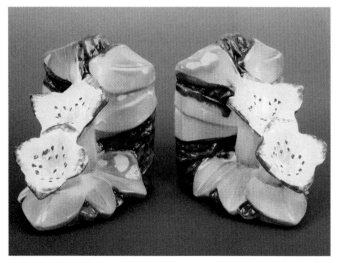

Lily bookends, 1940s, McCoy Made in USA mark, 6" tall. **$125-$150/pair**

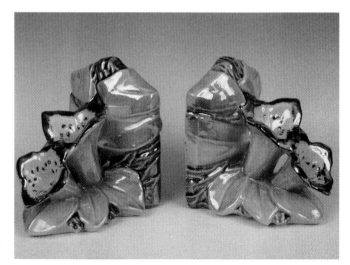

Lily bookends with pearly glaze in gold trim, 1940s to '50s, sometimes marked McCoy USA, usually unmarked, 5 1/2" tall. **$225-$275/pair**

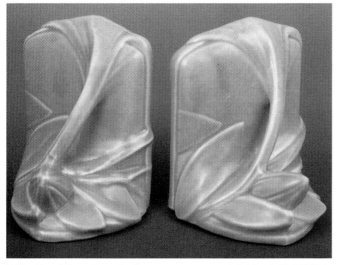

Lily Bud bookends in matte aqua, 1940s, NM USA mark, 5 3/4" tall. **$200-$250/pair**

Parakeets (also called Lovebirds) bookends in matte aqua, early 1940s, NM mark. **$200-$250/pair**

Swallow bookends/planters, 1950s, McCoy USA mark, 6" tall. **$275-$325/pair**

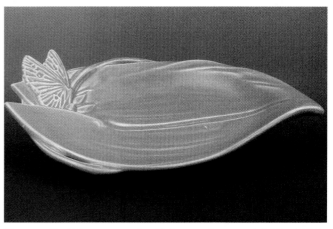

Butterfly Line console dish or platter, 1940s, NM USA mark, found in other matte colors, 14" long. **$350-$400**

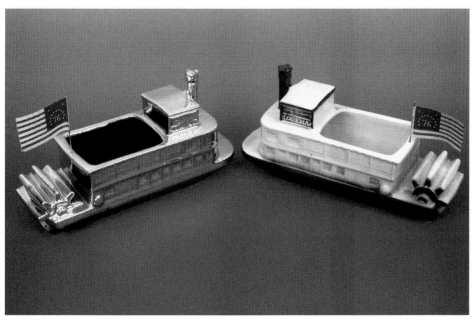

Commemorative steamboats (the "Lorena") made for Zanesville Chamber of Commerce, 1976, 7" long; **$70-$80 each**

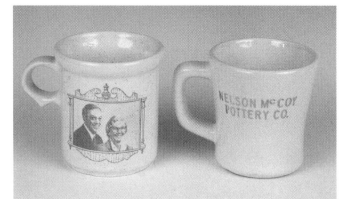

Left, **Nelson and Billie McCoy retirement mug**, 1981. **$100-$125** Right, **Nelson McCoy Pottery Co. mug**. **$80-$90**

Two **Butterfly Line pin dishes** (also called console bowls) in matte blue and yellow, 1940s, NM USA mark, 5" diameter. **$55-$65 each**

Pickling crock and butter churn, with original tag and dasher, Lancaster Colony, 1980s, 12 1/2" tall. **$60-$70 each**

All three sizes of **Lily Bud console bowls**, including 8 1/2" size. **$65-$75**

Lily Bud console bowls in 5 1/2" and 11 1/2" widths, 1940s, NM mark. 5 1/2", **$40-$50**; 11 1/2", **$125-$150** Two Lily Bud candleholders in matte aqua, 1940s, NM mark, 5 1/2" diameter. **$75-$85/pair**

Lily Bud 8 1/2" console bowl in matte lavender. **$65-$75**

Console bowl with candleholders, stoneware, late 1930s, more common in green, bowl 8" diameter. **$350-$450/set** (in green, **$200/set**)

Cuspidor with grapes motif in glossy brown, 1940s, unmarked, 7 1/2" diameter. **$50-$60**

Three-section Leaf candy or snack dish, early 1950s, McCoy mark, 11" wide, also found in Rustic glazes of green and brown. As shown, **$100-$125**; Rustic, **$50-$60**

Cupid Pig pitcher (model for smaller commemorative issued by McCoy Collection), only the second in this size known to exist, with damage, 9" tall. **$500-$700**

Leaf dish, ex-Cope Collection, unmarked, 12" long. **$1,200+**

Left, **Fawn flower bowl ornament** (one of the "ladder pieces," so named because they were pictured in an early McCoy guide on a drying rack that was tiered like the steps of a ladder), 1940s to 1950s, usually found in white or brown glaze, this one is ex-Ty Kuhn collection and painted by Kuhn. As shown, **$175-$200**; normally, **$90-$110**

Trinket box in atypical glaze, 1970s, McCoy USA mark, ex-Ty Kuhn collection. **$90-$110**

Lid from a covered casserole in the form of a long-billed bird with crest, lid also found in glossy brown but without crest. **No established value.**

Double Giraffe vase, not produced, a green and tan example is in the Cope Gallery in Roseville, Ohio; McCoy mark, 9 1/2" tall. **$5000**

Double candleholder, 1930s (?), raised McCoy mark but not a production piece, 9 1/2" tall, only two others known to exist in the Cope Gallery. **$3000 to $5,000**

Miniature teapot with hand-painted decoration under glaze on raised grape design, this variation was never produced, but a similar pot with flat decoration was made, 3 1/2" tall. **$300-$350** Ceramic plaque designed for use as a pin, but without pin back, ex-Cope Collection. **Not a product of McCoy**

Money chest bank, replicating a box from the Bowery Savings Bank, late 1960s, no mark, 6" wide, **$35-$40**

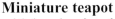

Glaze screen, cast iron with mesh, used to screen glaze compounds, and trimming knife used to clean unfired pottery after removal from molds.
Knife: $125, Screen: $200

Fish flower bowl ornament (one of a kind?), 1950s, USA mark, 4 1/2" tall, **$2,300+**

Double Angelfish and Seahorses flower bowl ornaments or aquarium decorations, 1940s, unmarked, 6" and 6 1/4" tall, also found in green. Fish, **$200-$250**; Seahorses, **$300-$350**

Four **flower bowl ornaments** (the witch, gnome, and pelican are "ladder pieces," so named because they were pictured in an early McCoy guide on a drying rack that was tiered like the steps of a ladder), 1940s to 1950s, usually found in white or brown (rare) glaze, USA or unmarked, about 3" tall. Cat and witch, **$400-$450**; Gnome, **$300-$325**; Pelican, **$400-$425**

Three **flower bowl ornaments** or flower holders (fish), 1940s to 1950s, usually found in white, yellow, green, or brown glaze, USA or unmarked. Fish, 3" tall, **$150-$200**; Rabbit, 1 1/2" tall, **$300-$350**

Two **key minders**, 1960s, **$50-$70 each**

Foreground, **console bowl** with applied grapes in gold trim, 1950s, McCoy USA and Shafer marks and an employee stamp "Z," 12" long. **$60-$75**
Gondola candy dish in gold trim, this example has the oar support, which is missing on some dishes, 1950s, McCoy mark, 11 1/2" long. **$60-$75**

Hands novelty dish (sometimes called an ashtray) in gold trim, 1940s, NM USA mark, 5 3/4" long. **$70-$80**

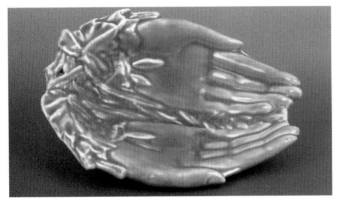

Large Hands novelty dish in glossy aqua, 1940s, NM USA mark, 8 1/2" long. **$125-$150**

GOP convention commemorative (1956?), unmarked, 5 1/2" tall. **$90-$110**

Five **flower bowl ornaments** in matte white (the first four from left are "ladder pieces," so named because they were pictured in an early McCoy guide on a drying rack that was tiered like the steps of a ladder), 1940s, usually found in white or brown (rare) glaze, unmarked, from 3 3/4" to 4 3/4" tall. **$100-$125 each**

Ashtray, a lunch-hour piece, with applied heart and the words "MA" and "PA," marked McCoy on reverse, made from the bottom of a Cornucopia vase, 6 1/2" by 3 1/4". **$200-$300**

Christmas items: left, covered jar dated 1973, 5 3/4" tall; right, coffee mug dated 1967 and marked "The Kuhns," 5" tall. **$30-$40 each**

Two **Brocade pieces**: round covered dish and trinket box, possibly part of a dresser set, 1950s, McCoy USA 464 mark. **$80-$90/pair**

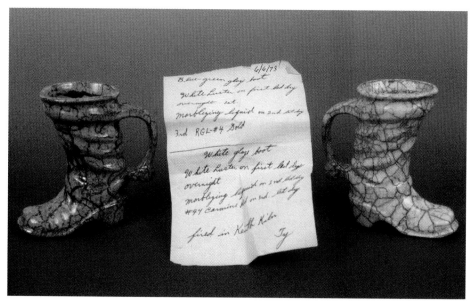

Two **Cowboy Boot pencil holders,** 1973, normally brown, these are in test glazes with formula notes by Ty Kuhn, 5" tall. **$100 each**

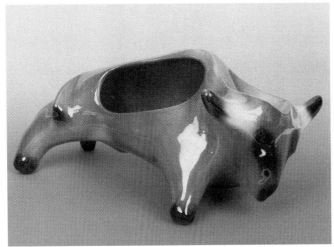

Bull dresser caddie made for Swank, 1960s, unmarked, 10" long. **$25-$35**

Lion dresser caddie made for Swank, 1960s, unmarked, 10" long. **$55-$65**

Racehorse dresser caddie made for Swank with clothes brush tail, 1960s, unmarked, 9" long not including tail. **$75-$85**

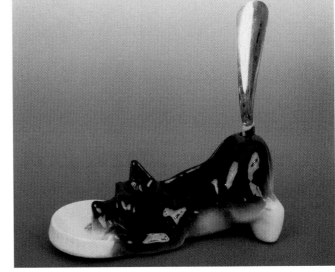

Dog dresser caddie made for Swank with shoehorn tail, 1960s, unmarked, 11" long. **$45-$55**

Non-production nut dish in leaves motif, McCoy mark, only a dozen known to exist. **$300-$350**

1932 Pierce Arrow decanter made for Jim Beam, 1960s, McCoy mark, 11" long. **$75-$85**

Lion statue, 1960s, unmarked, 15" long. **$45-$55**

Inhaler replica, 9" tall. **$30-$35**

Left, **Hung-over dog bank** made for Swank, 1960s, unmarked, 6" tall; right, **Eagle bank,** 1960s, unmarked, 7" tall. **$50-$60 each**

Baseball glove and ball desk piece (?), 1950s, unmarked. **$40-$50**

Two **Grecian Line console bowls** (8" and 12" diameter, McCoy USA mark, number 444) and **candleholders** (4" diameter, unmarked), 1950s. 12" bowl, **$80-$90**; 8", **$50-$60**; Candleholders, **$90-$110/pair**

Mini jug in deep forest green, 1960s, unmarked. **$20-$25**

McCoy advertised a variety of ceramic figures with cutout faces for the Halloween season.

Smiling jack-o'-lanterns and ghosts by McCoy were included in a Halloween display.

McCoy Limited
26 North Third Street, Zanesville, OH 43701
614/453-6048 or 453-0654

608MB

615MB

610MB

613MB

606MB

609MB

620M

Several sizes of turkey figures and a cornucopia were among Thanksgiving items produced by McCoy.

Spirit of 76

28-0348-73 28-0367-73 28-0340-73 28-0380-73 28-0355-73

28-0335-73 28-0334-73 Set

28-0359-73 28-0330-73 28-0331-73 28-0332-73 28-0333-73

28-0343-73 28-0342-73 28-0341-73

28-0381-73
28-0382-73
28-0383-73

28-0350-73

28-0369-73 28-0351-73

McCoy's Spirit of 76 line of pots, jars, jugs, and even a bell, honored the U.S. Bicentennial in 1976.

McCoy introduced a line of Schlitz beer steins in its 1973 catalog.

Steins with nearly two dozen designs and decorations were featured in a 1973 McCoy catalog.

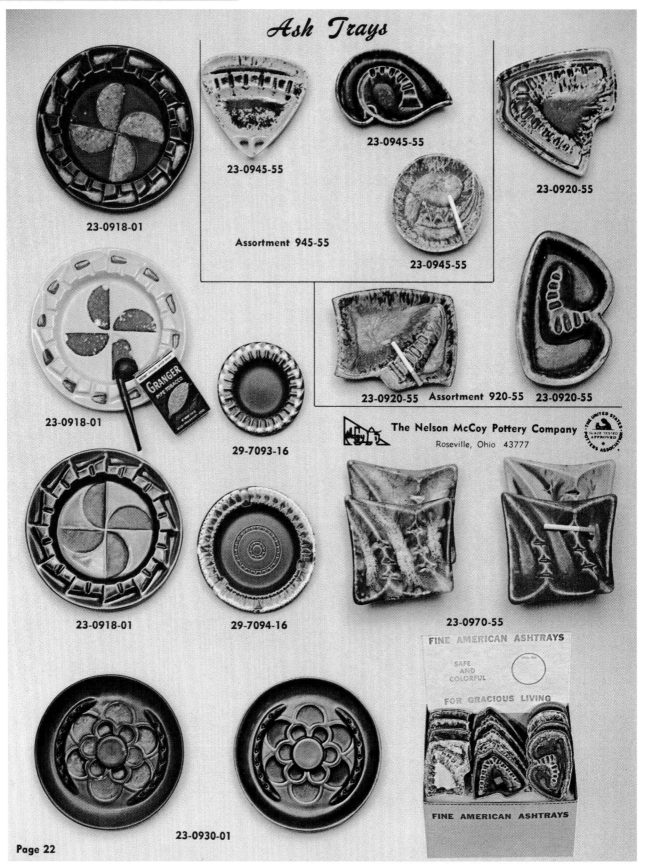

Ash Trays

23-0918-01

23-0945-55

23-0945-55

23-0920-55

Assortment 945-55

23-0945-55

23-0918-01

23-0920-55   Assortment 920-55   23-0920-55

GRANGER PIPE TOBACCO

29-7093-16

The Nelson McCoy Pottery Company
Roseville, Ohio 43777

23-0918-01

29-7094-16

23-0970-55

FINE AMERICAN ASHTRAYS

SAFE AND COLORFUL

FOR GRACIOUS LIVING

23-0930-01

FINE AMERICAN ASHTRAYS

Page 22

Among McCoy products advertised in 1973 were several types of ashtrays called "safe and colorful for gracious living."

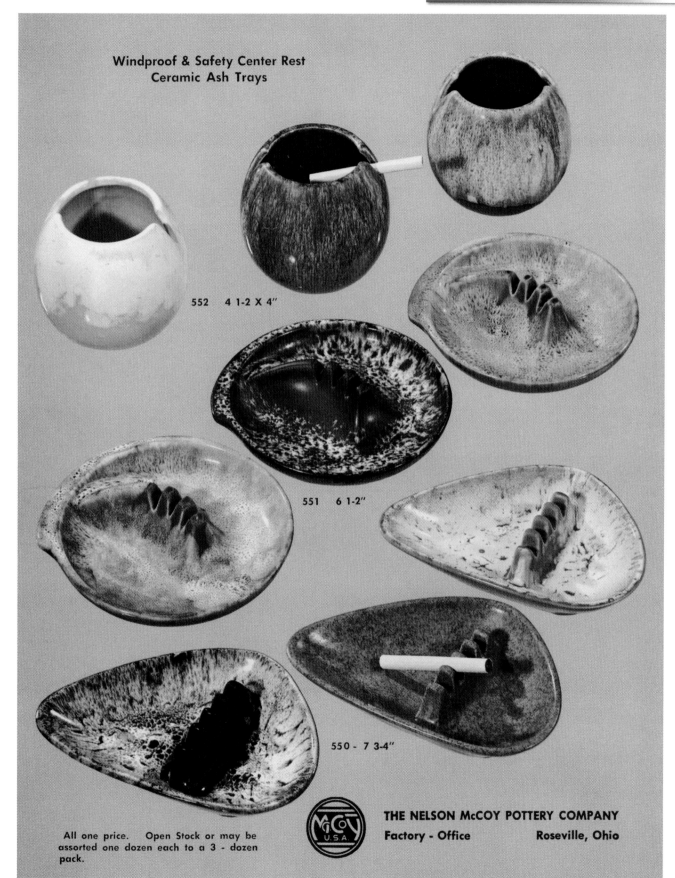

**Windproof & Safety Center Rest
Ceramic Ash Trays**

552   4 1-2 X 4"

551   6 1-2"

550 - 7 3-4"

All one price.   Open Stock or may be assorted one dozen each to a 3 - dozen pack.

THE NELSON McCOY POTTERY COMPANY
Factory - Office   **Roseville, Ohio**

Ceramic ashtrays in several colors and styles were "Windproof & Safety Center Rest," McCoy said.

(A) 144G, 144S
HOLLY LEAF (with votive drop-in)
2¾" x 5¾" dark green w/red
berries, pk. 12, wt. 10 lbs.
~~$3~~ 2.50

(B) 146G, 146S
**HOLLY PEDESTAL (uses large
red pillar candle)**
pk. 24, wt. 12 lbs.
$2.50

(C) 141W
CROSS (small)
cut out for use with votive,
10½" x 6¼," pk. 6, 10 lbs.
$6.00

*(D) 138W, 138S
**SANTA (holes star-shaped for use
with votive)**
white glaze or sandstone,
6" x 4," pk. 12, wt. 12 lbs.
Glaze-$4.00, Sandstone-$3.50.

*(E) 139CTW, 139CTS
MRS. SANTA (candle top)
white glaze or sandstone,
5¾" x 3½," pk. 12, wt. 12 lbs.
Glaze-$4.00, Sandstone-$3.50.

(F) 140M
LARGE SNOWMAN (decorated)
7" x 5," pk. 6, wt. 9 lbs.
$5.00

*(G) 139W, 139S
**MRS. SANTA (holes star-shaped
for use with votive)**
white glaze or sandstone,
5¾" x 3½," pk. 12, wt. 12 lbs.
Glaze-$4.00, Sandstone-$3.50.

(H) M137G, M137W, M137S
CHRISTMAS TREE (large)
9½" x 9" Green or white tipped
w/green, pk. 6, wt. 20 lbs.
~~$8.95~~ 7.95

*(I) 138CTW, 138CTS
SANTA (candle top)
white glaze or sandstone,
6" x 4," pk. 12, wt. 12 lbs.
Glaze-$4.00, Sandstone-$3.50.

McCoy Limited advertised "Christmas Scarf People" and ceramic Christmas trees as part of its holiday line.

*(J) 155W, 155S
SNOWGIRL (small)
cut out for use with votive,
white glaze or sandstone,
5" x 4¼," pk. 12, wt. 11 lbs.
Glaze-$4.00, Sandstone-$3.50.

*(K) 145W, 145S
SNOWBOY (small)
cut out for use with votive,
white glaze or sandstone,
6" x 4¼," pk. 12, wt. 11 lbs.
Glaze-$4.00, Sandstone-$3.50.

(L) X4
LINDSAY PLATE AND MUG
pk. 6, wt. 10 lbs.
$4.00

(M) M111G, M111W, M111S
WEE TREE
green or white tipped w/green
3½," pk. 24, wt. 15 lbs.
$2.25

(N) M115G, M115W, M115S
CHRISTMAS TREE (small)
6½" x 6," white tipped w/green,
green or sandstone
pk. 12, wt. 14 lbs.
$3.95

(O) 1BU
BASE CORD UNIT
(base, electrical cord, bulb)
pk. 12, wt. 5 lbs.
$3.50

(P) 1LU
LIGHT UNIT
(electrical cord, bulb only)
pk. 12, wt. 3 lbs.
~~$2.00~~ 1.50

(Q) 160M
CANDLE PLATE
6½," pk. 24, wt. 20 lbs.
$1.80

PRICES EFFECTIVE March 15, 1985
F.O.B. Roseville, OH. Terms: Net 30 Days
Add 10% for UPS Shipment.

*with red scarf.

Western WW Ware

0933 4000
Ash Tray

0935 4000
16 oz. Mug

0934 4000
10 oz. Mug

0938 4000
Grub Box

0937 4000
Snack Bowl

0939 4000
7" Boot Vase

0936 4000
2½ qt. Pitcher

Nelson McCoy
A Lancaster Colony Company
Nelson McCoy Pottery Company
Roseville, Ohio 43777

An ashtray, mugs, and even a cowboy boots vase were part of Nelson McCoy's Western Ware line.

SOMETHING DIFFERENT?
TRY
"Chocolate Bisque"

A novelty planter and jardiniere group in an eye-catching brown bisque finish outside with green or yellow gloss interiors.

No. 551—6 x 4" Golf Planter
Brown Spray w/Yellow or
Green Interior Dec.
Pkd. 1 Doz. Wt. 20 lbs.
$14.40 per Doz.

No. 552—6 x 4½"
Fisherman Planter
Brown Spray w/Yellow or
Green Interior Dec.
Pkd. 1 Doz. Wt. 20 lbs.
$14.40 per Doz.

No. 553—6½ x 4"
Bowling Planter
Brown Spray w/Yellow or
Green Interior Dec.
Pkd. 1 Doz. Wt. 20 lbs.
$14.40 per Doz.

No. 554—6 x 6"
Baseball Planter
Brown Spray w/Yellow or
Green Interior Dec.
Pkd. 1 Doz. Wt. 22 lbs.
$14.40 per Doz.

 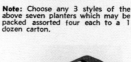

No. 555—6½ x 5½"
Boxing Glove Planter
Brown Spray w/Yellow or
Green Interior Dec.
Pkd. 1 Doz. Wt. 17 lbs.
$14.40 per Doz.

No. 559—7" Football Planter
Brown Spray w/Yellow or
Green Interior Dec.
Pkd. 1 Doz. Wt. 17 lbs.
$14.40 per Doz.

No. 558—7½ x 5"
Cradle Planter
Brown Spray w/ Pink or
Blue Interior Dec.
Pkd. 1 Doz. Wt. 22 lbs.
$14.40 per Doz.

Note: Choose any 3 styles of the above seven planters which may be packed assorted four each to a 1 dozen carton.

No. 748—9 x 4½"
Automobile Planter
Brown Spray w/Yellow
or Green Interior Dec.
Pkd. 1 Doz. Wt. 36 lbs.
$21.20 per Doz.

No. 750—9½ x 4½"
Convertible Auto Planter
Brown Spray w/Yellow
or Green Interior Dec.
Pkd. 1 Doz. Wt. 36 lbs.
$21.20 per Doz.

No. 619—6¾"
Window Box
Brown Spray w/Yellow or
Green Interior
Pkd. 2 Doz. Wt. 28 lbs.
$10.40 per Doz.

Note: The Nos. 748 and 750 automobiles may be packed assorted ½ Doz. ea. to a 1 dozen carton.

No. 631—8¾" Log Planter
Brown Spray w/Yellow or
Green Interior Dec.
Pkd. 1 Doz. Wt. 23 lbs.
$14.40 per Doz.

No. 500—9" Planting Dish
Brown Spray w/Yellow or
Green Interior
Pkd. 1 Doz. Wt. 25 lbs.
$14.40 per Doz.

No. 49—Jardiniere
Sizes 6½"-7½"
Brown Spray w/Yellow or
Green Interior. Also solid
White or Green
6½"—$16.00 per Doz. 1 Doz. 32 lbs.
7½"—$17.60 per Doz. 1 Doz. 42 lbs.

No. 4PJ—11" Porch Jar
Brown Spray w/Yellow or
Green Interior. Also solid
White or Green
Pkd. 1/3 Doz. Wt. 37 lbs.
$3.60 Each

The Nelson-McCoy Pottery Company . . . Roseville, Ohio

Planters, jars, and a window box from the Chocolate Bisque novelty line by McCoy.

Dual Purpose Candle Holders

34-0020-01

34-0090-01

34-0073-01

34-0073-01

The Nelson McCoy Pottery Company
Subsidiary of Mount Clemens China Company
Roseville, Ohio 43777

34-0089-01

34-0071-01

| 34-0096-54 | 34-0099-54 | 34-0095-54 | 34-0093-54 | 34-0098-54 | 34-0097-54 | 36-0094-54 |

ASSORTMENT 34-0100-54

Page 19

Designs and colors varied widely in McCoy's line of Dual Purpose Candle Holders in a 1972 catalog.

THE "GOLDEN BROCADE" LINE
24 Carat Gold Effect

No. 6051

No. 6052

No. 6055

TARNISH PROOF
24 CARAT GOLD
EFFECT
GOLDEN BROCADE
By McCOY
MADE IN U.S.A.
WASH IN LUKEWARM SOAP WATER

No. 6056

Giftware

GOLDEN

BROCADE

for Gracious Living

No. 6053

No. 6054

No. 6071

No. 6057

No. 6066

No. 6059

No. 6060

No. 6072

No. 6058

The Nelson McCoy Pottery Company
Subsidiary of Mount Clemens Pottery Company
Area Code 614 697-7331   Roseville, Ohio 43777

Page 7

McCoy's Golden Brocade line offered a "24 Carat Gold Effect" in giftware, including serving dishes, vases, and candle holders.

28-0301-73

28-0273-08

39-1369-86

39-1378-86

28-0297-08

28-0292-08

28-0294-08

28-0293-08

28-0314-73

28-0290-17

50-0529-08

25

There was no shortage of selections available in mugs from McCoy in a 1977 catalog.

MUGS

Some of the many mugs available in a McCoy 1976 catalog were in patriotic themes, reflecting the U.S. Bicentennial.

Pet Feeders

Some forms of McCoy pet feeders are being reproduced, and some potteries are still making dishes in vintage styles. So look for age signs like glaze crazing, discolored bases that may have an unglazed—or "dry"—foot ring, and compare weights, since old pieces are almost always heavier than later versions.

Though sometimes called pet feeders, these three **Stoneware dishes with Parading Elephants** are also known as bulb bowls, 1920s. Green is the most common glaze (**$60-$70; blue, $80-$90; yellow, $100+**); they have an unglazed or "dry" rim, and come with two bases, low (McCoy shield mark 87) and raised with a fluted border and tripod feet (Brush McCoy, unmarked).

Left, **new dog dish** (dogs running to right, lighter weight, brighter glaze). Right, slightly different **Bird Dog dish** in green glaze, 7 1/2" diameter. **$75-$90**

Two versions of the **Hunting Dog feeder** with raised dog pattern, one with a dry rim and one glazed, 1930s, unmarked, 6 1/2" diameter. **$75-$90 each**

Cat and Dog feeders, 1940s, McCoy mark, 6" diameter. **$75-$90 each**

Two sizes of **dog dishes,** with decals, 1970s, McCoy Mt. Clemens mark, 7" and 6 3/4" diameter. **$90-$110 each**

Four **"To Man's Best Friend, His Dog" bowls** showing glaze and mold variations (dry rim is earlier), 1930s and '40s, McCoy Made in USA mark, 7 1/2" diameter. **$75-$90**

Left, two **"To Man's Best Friend, His Dog" bowls** showing bottom mark. Right, reproduction bowl, 6" diameter.

Three "Dog. (Period)" bowls, also called Spaniel feeders because the tapered design kept the dog's ears out of the bowl, 1940s, McCoy mark or unmarked, 6 1/2" diameter. **$75-$90 each**

Dog feeder, 1940s, glazed bottom, unmarked, 5" diameter. **$50-$60**

Pet feeder, UNIPET treat bowl with bell in lid, late 1960s, UNIPET Upjohn mark. **$45-$55**

Jardinieres

Jardinieres & Peds

Pet Feeders

No. 421C—6" Sq. Jardiniere
Amethyst inside—Pink outside
Mustard inside—Brown outside
Packed 1 Doz. Wt. 23 lbs.
$14.40 per Dozen

No. 412—7½" Jardiniere
Brown Spray or Green Spray
Packed 1 Doz. Wt. 42 lbs.
$17.60 per Dozen

No. 47—7½" Jardiniere
Yellow or White
Packed 1 Doz. Wt. 52 lbs.
$14.40 per Dozen

No. 58 Jardiniere
Sizes 4½"-5½"-6½"-7½"-
8½"-9½"-10½"
Green, White, Yellow

4½"—$ 6.70 per Doz.	3 Doz.	37 lbs.
5½"—$ 8.40 per Doz.	2 Doz.	40 lbs.
6½"—$10.20 per Doz.	1½ Doz.	42 lbs.
7½"—$14.40 per Doz.	1½ Doz.	42 lbs.
8½"—$20.00 per Doz.	2/3 Doz.	37 lbs.
9½"—$24.60 per Doz.	2/3 Doz.	50 lbs.
10½"—$32.00 per Doz.	1/3 Doz.	36 lbs.

No. 48—Jardinieres
Sizes 8½"-10½"
Green or White
8½"—$20.00 per Doz. 2/3 Doz. 47 lbs.
10½"—$32.00 per Doz. 1/3 Doz. 40 lbs.

No. 48—Jar and Ped.
Green and White
8½" Jard. and 12½" Pedestal
1 only—18 lbs.
$5.30 each

No. 3—10" Porch Jar
White or Green
Packed 1/3 Doz. Wt. 57 lbs.
Available with or without
Drainage—please specify
$4.00 each

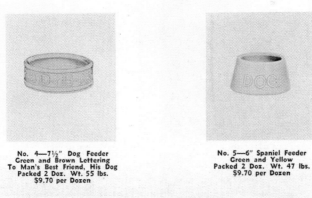

No. 4—7½" Dog Feeder
Green and Brown Lettering
To Man's Best Friend, His Dog
Packed 2 Doz. Wt. 55 lbs.
$9.70 per Dozen

No. 5—6" Spaniel Feeder
Green and Yellow
Packed 2 Doz. Wt. 47 lbs.
$9.70 per Dozen

A dog feeder and a spaniel feeder were included in a 1958 McCoy catalog.

Planters

Many collectors believe that planters represent the most varied and entertaining area of McCoy wares. From the simple leaf forms to the elaborate figural pieces featuring birds and animals, look for examples with crisp molds and good cold-paint or gilt trim. Check closely for damage or signs of restoration, especially on planters with applied birds and flowers.

Bird planting dish, 1950s, McCoy mark, 10" wide. **$25-$35**

Goat planter, 1950s, McCoy mark, USA mark. **$300-$350**

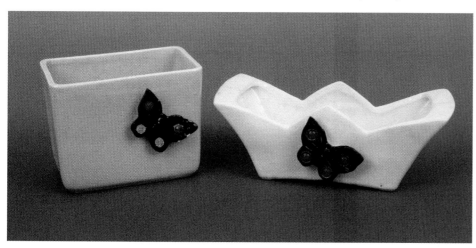

Two **Jewel Line planters** with applied butterflies, 1950s, McCoy USA mark. **$110-$125 each**

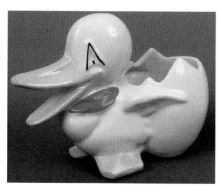

Duck and Egg planter with cold paint, 1950s, McCoy Made in USA mark, 3 1/2" tall. **$35-$45**

Left, **round planting dish,** McCoy mark, 7" diameter. **$25-$35** Right, **window box,** McCoy USA mark, 8 1/2" long. **$35-$45**

Leaves and Berries planter with hand-painted decoration under glaze, 1950s, McCoy USA mark, 5" tall. **$45-$55**

Left, **Rocking chair planter,** with cold paint, 1950s, McCoy USA mark, 8 1/2" tall. **$50-$60** Right, **Chinaman planter,** 1950s, McCoy USA mark, 5 1/2" tall. **$25-$30**

Floraline rock planter, 1960s, marked "Floraline 553 Lancaster USA," 8 1/2" long. **$45-$55**

Three **Floraline footed planters,** 1960s, style numbers 434 and T-519, all 7" diameter. **$12-$18 each**

Antelope planter, 1950s, unmarked, 12" long. **$400-$450**

Two **Antelope window boxes** (also called ferneries) in matte white and aqua, 1940s, NM mark (hard to find) and unmarked, come with grooved rim and without, 9 1/2" long. White, **$90-$110**; Aqua, **$45-$55**

Two **Antique Rose pieces** in blue with transfer decoration: watering can and swan planter, each 7" tall, 1959, McCoy USA mark. **$45-$60 each** Also found in white with red or brown rose.

Two **Butterfly Line hanging basket planters** in matte blue and aqua, 1940s, NM mark, found with and without holes, 6 1/2" diameter. **$200-$225 each**

Two **Butterfly Line trough planters** or window boxes in matte aqua and blue, 1940s, NM USA mark, 8 1/4" long. **$65-$75 each**

Butterfly Line window box in matte aqua, 1940s, unmarked, hard to find this size, 9 1/4" long. **$150-$175** (if marked, **$250**)

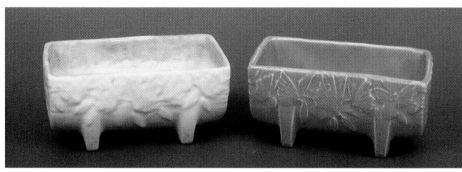

Two **Butterfly Line trough planters,** 1940s, NM USA mark, 5 1/2" long. **$35-$45 each**

Planters

Two **Butterfly Line planters** in matte aqua. Left, unmarked butterfly, 1940s, 7 1/2" wide. **$125-$150** Right, ivy planter, 1940s, USA mark, 4" tall. **$65-$75**

Flying ducks planter in natural colors, 1950s, McCoy USA mark, 10" wide. **$175-$225**

Flying ducks planter in raspberry and chartreuse, 1950s, McCoy USA mark, 10" wide. **$175-$225**

Two **garden dishes** or window boxes in matte blue and aqua, early 1940s, NM USA mark, rare, 9 1/4" long. **$110-$125**

Two **planters.** Left, 1950s, McCoy USA mark, 9" long. **$25-$35** Right, 1940s, McCoy USA mark, 8 1/4" long. **$55-$65**

Bird dog planter, 1950s, McCoy USA mark, also found in chartreuse with a black or brown dog, 8 1/2" tall. **$175-$225**

Two **trough planters** or window boxes in matte aqua and blue, 1940s, NM USA mark, 7" long. **$45-$55 each**

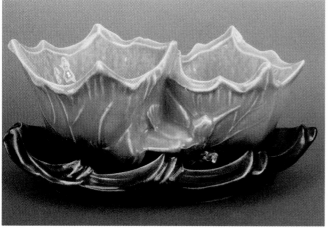

Humming Bird planter in blue, late 1940s, McCoy USA mark, 10 1/2" wide. **$125-$150**

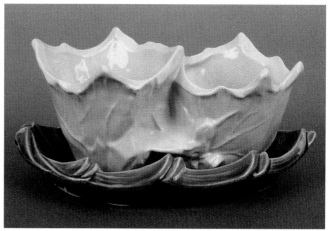

Humming Bird planter in green, late 1940s, McCoy USA mark, 10 1/2" wide. **$125-$150**

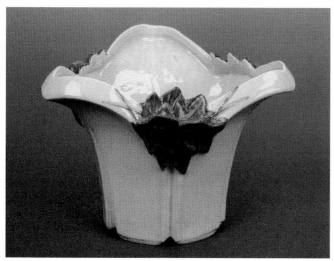

Three-sided ivy planter, 1950s, McCoy USA mark, hard to find, 6" tall. **$400-$500**

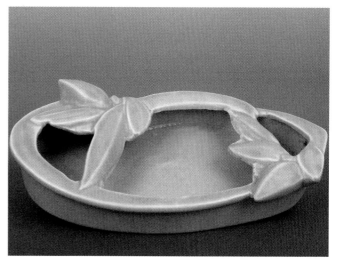

Lily Bud divided planting dish in matte aqua, 1940s, NM USA mark, 11 1/2" long. **$85-$95**

Planters

Two **Lily Bud planting dishes** in matte aqua, 1940s, NM USA mark. Left, 9" long, **$65-$75** Right, 8" long (called the cross), **$65-$75**

Low planting dish with drape design in matte aqua, 1940s, NM USA mark, 8 1/2" diameter. **$65-$75** (rarely found without inverted lip).

Two **window boxes** in matte aqua and blue, 1940s, NM USA, 8 1/4" long. **$65-$75 each**

Grapes window box in matte aqua (rare), 1940s, NM USA mark, 10" long. **$110-$125**

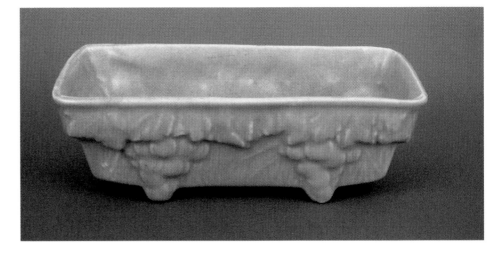

Two **Sand Butterfly trough planters** in matte aqua and glossy coral, 1930s, USA mark, 8 3/4" long. Matte colors, **$50-$65**; Coral, **$65+**

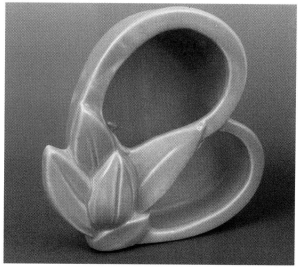

Lily Bud divided planting dish in matte blue, 1940s, NM USA mark, 6 1/2" wide. **$65-$75** right, Lily Bud pillow vase in matte aqua, 1940s, NM USA mark, 6 1/2" tall, **$75 to $85**

Left, **Lily Bud "twig" planter** in matte aqua, 1940s, NM USA mark, 5" tall. **$90-$110** Right, **Lily Bud "banana boat" planter** in matte aqua, NM USA mark, 8 1/2" long. **$55-$65**

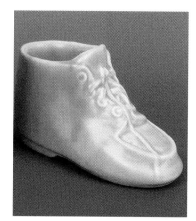

Mary Jane shoe planter in matte aqua, 1940s, NM USA mark. **$35-$45**

Left, **Strawberry planter** in matte blue, stoneware, 1930s, unmarked, 6 1/2" tall. **$85-$95** Right, **Shell planter** in matte aqua, also found in glossy colors, 1940s, NM USA mark, 7 1/2" long. **$55-$65**

Planters

Left, **Baby Crib planter,** part of the Nursery Line, 1950s, unmarked, 6 1/2" long. **$30-$40** Right, **hanging Strawberry planter,** 1950s, McCoy USA mark, 6" tall. **$50-$60**

Swan planter in matte aqua, 1940s, unmarked, 5" tall. **$45-$55**

Left, **Cornucopia planter** with tassels in matte yellow, 1940s, McCoy mark, 8" tall. **$55-$65** Right, **hanging basket planter,** stoneware, 1930s, unmarked, 7" diameter. **$85-$95**

Bird of Paradise planter in glossy white (rarely found with cold-paint details), 1940s, McCoy mark, 13" long. **$55-$65**

Left, **Panda and Cradle planter,** 1940s, McCoy USA mark, some pandas and blankets are cold painted, 5 1/2" tall. **$110-$125** Right, **Bonnet Duck and Egg planter,** 1940s, McCoy mark, cold paint, 5 3/4" tall. **$175-$225**

Two **Pussy at the Well planters,** 1950s, McCoy USA mark, 7" tall. **$125-$150 each**

Single cache planter in black and pink, 1950s, McCoy USA mark, 9" wide. **$70-$80**

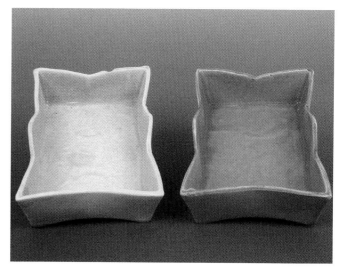

Two **planting dishes** in matte pink and aqua, 1940s, NM USA mark, 9" long. **$35-$40 each**

Planters

Three **figural planters** in glossy aqua: left, Singing Bird, 1940s, unmarked, found in other colors, 4 1/2" tall. **$30-$40** Parrot, 1940s, NM USA mark, also found in pink and white, 7" tall. **$40-$50** Right, Backwards Bird, 1940s, NM USA mark, also found in white and yellow, 4 1/2" tall. **$60-$70**

Blossomtime planters in matte white, 1940s, McCoy mark, (also found in yellow), 6" and 5" tall. **$50-$75 each**

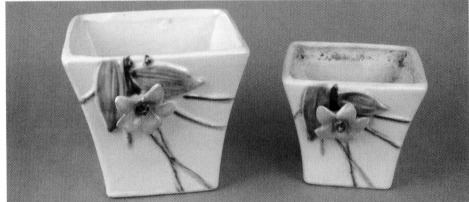

Singing Bird planter in matte white, 1940s, USA mark, found in other colors, 4 1/2" tall. **$30-$40** (also found in 6 3/4" size).

Two versions of the **Rabbit planter,** yellow version never had cold paint, 1950s, McCoy mark, 7 1/4" tall. **$100-$150 each,** depending on paint condition.

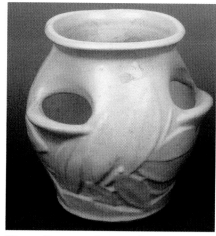

Strawberry planter in matte white, stoneware, 1930s, unmarked, 6 1/2" tall. **$60-$70**

Two **Snowman planters** with cold-painted details, late 1940s, McCoy mark, 6" tall. **$70-$90 each,** depending on paint condition.

Log planter with gold trim, 1950s, McCoy mark, also found in green, 12 1/2" long. **$110-$125** with gold trim. Without, **$80-$90**

Petal basket planter, 1950s, McCoy USA mark, 8 3/4" tall. **$150-$175**

Pine cone planter, mid-1940s, McCoy USA mark, 8" wide, rare. **$500-$600** (A slightly larger planter in rust glaze, **$1,800-$2,000**)

Planters

Turtle planter with lily pad in atypical glaze (often found with yellow cold-paint decoration), early 1950s, McCoy mark, 8" long. Normally, **$60-$70;** As shown, **$150-$200**

Two **hanging basket planters,** in brown and green and matte white, 1930s, unmarked, 6" diameter. **$70-$90 each**

Left, **Scoop planter** in forest green, late 1950s, McCoy mark, 6" wide. **$25-$35** Right, **low Vine planter** with under-glaze decoration, mid-1950s, McCoy mark, 8 1/2" wide. **$35-$45**

Two forms of **Strawberry planters,** one in atypical dusty burgundy, one in glossy green, stoneware, 1930s, unmarked, 7" tall. **$60-$70 each** (This form is also found with a raised leaf motif on the body, called style #2.)

Square textured planters in glossy green, interlocking, 1950s, unmarked, 3 1/2" and 5" tall. **$25-$30 each**

Village Smithy planter in atypical burgundy and gray (usually in brown and green), 1950s, McCoy USA mark. As shown, **$300-$350;** In common glaze, **$70-$80**

Large Turtle planter, 1950s, McCoy mark, 12 1/2" long. **$125-$150** (also found in other color combinations see p.197)

Two **Harmony boat planters,** early 1960s, McCoy mark, also found in orange and a brighter yellow, 8 1/2" and 9 1/2" long. **$25-$30 each**

Left, **Harmony boat planter** in gold trim, 1960s, McCoy USA mark, 12" long. **$40-$50** Right, **Crestwood footed planter,** 1960s, McCoy USA mark, 4 1/2" tall. **$40-$50**

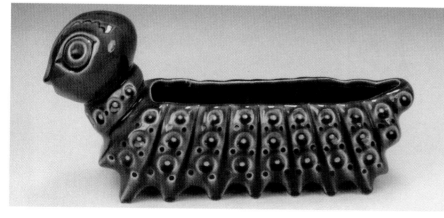

Caterpillar planter, 1960s, Floraline mark, 13 1/2" long, also found in brown, white, and yellow. **$40-$50**

Snail planter, 1960s, Floraline mark. **$40-$50**

Turtle planter, 1960s, Floraline mark. **$40-$50**

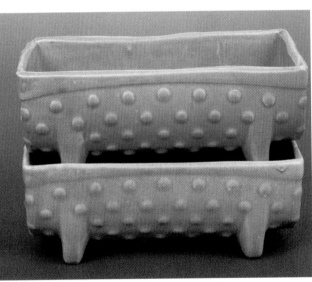

Two **Hobnail trough planters** in matte blue and aqua, 1940s, NM USA mark, 8 1/2" long. **$50-$60 each**

Small Hobnail planter in matte aqua, early 1940s, unmarked, probably a cut-down vase, 3 1/4" tall. **No established value.**

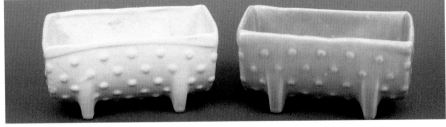

Two **Hobnail trough planters** in matte white and aqua, 1940s, NM USA mark, 5 1/2" long. **$30-$40 each**

Left, **square-top Hobnail planter** in matte aqua, 1940s, NM USA mark, 4" tall. **$55-$65** Right, **Ball planter** in glossy aqua (also called rose bowl), 1940s, NM USA mark, 3 1/2" tall. **$45-$55**

Two **Floraline planters**—bear and turtle—in glossy brown glaze, 1960s, Floraline mark (may also be marked USA or McCoy), each 3 1/2" tall. **$15-$20 each**

Three **animal planters**—kitten, puppy, and fawn—in pearly gray and rustic brown (glazes may vary), 1970s, marks include McCoy USA LCC and USA, with serial numbers 3026, 3027, and 3028, 6 3/4" to 7 1/2" tall. **$75-$90 each**

Three **fruit planters**—all oranges in varying glazes—1950s, McCoy USA mark, all 6 1/2" long. **$70-$90 each**

Three **fruit planters**—apple, pear, and grapes—1950s, McCoy USA mark, all 6 1/2" long. Apple and pear, **$60-$70 each;** Grapes, **$150-$175**

Three **fruit planters**—lemon, banana, and pomegranate—1950s, McCoy USA mark, all 6 1/2" long. Lemon and banana, **$100-$125 each;** Pomegranate, **$125-$150**

Left, **Mammy on Scoop planter** (also found with yellow scoop), cold-paint decoration, 1950s, McCoy mark, 7 1/2" long. **$175-$200** Right, **Boy on Rolling Pin planter** (also found with yellow pin), cold-paint decoration, 1950s, McCoy mark, 7 1/2" long. **$125-$150**

Bottom of **fruit planter** showing McCoy USA mark and employee letter stamp, "U."

Frog with Umbrella and **Duck with Umbrella planters,** mid-1950s, McCoy mark, with cold-paint decoration, 7 1/2" tall. **$150-$200 each**

Wash Tub Woman planter, not a production piece but marked NM, 6" tall, ex-Cope Collection, **with damage, $1000.**

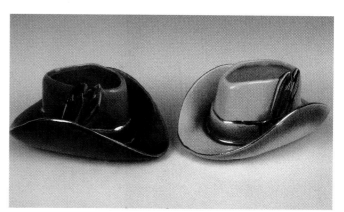

Left, **Calypso Line barrel planter,** late 1950s, McCoy mark, with cold-paint decoration, 5" tall. **$125-$150,** depending on paint condition. Right, **Donkey with Bananas planter,** 1950s, only one known to exist, 6" tall. **$1,500+**

Calypso Line Banana Boat planter, with cold-paint decoration (also found with all under-glaze color), late 1950s, McCoy mark, 11" long. **$175-$200**

Hat planters in brown and beige with gold trim, 1950s, McCoy USA and Shafer marks, 8" long. **$60-$75 each**

Pair of **ribbed and footed planters** in matte white, late 1940s, unmarked, 6" tall (also come in 8" size). **$70-$80/pair**

Three **animal planters** (cat with a bow, kittens with a basket, and puppy with turtle) in gold trim, 1950s, McCoy mark; kittens 7" tall. **$70-$80 each**

Planters

Left, **Liberty Bell planter** with gold trim, with 8th of July error (later corrected to 4th of July, rare), 1950s, McCoy USA mark, 8 1/4" tall. **$300-$350** Right, **Quail planter** in gold trim, 1950s, McCoy USA and Shafer mark, 7" tall. **$125-$150**

Left, **Kittens with basket planter** in gold trim in another glaze combination, 1950s, McCoy mark, 7" tall. **$70-$80** Right, **Grapes planter** in gold trim (rare), 1940s to '50s, McCoy USA mark, 6 1/2" long. **$275-$325**

Liberty Bell planter with correct date and black bell in cold paint. **$350-$400,** depending on paint condition

Left, **Alligator planter** in gold trim, 1950s, McCoy USA, 10" long. **$125-$150** Right, **Pedestal planter** in gold trim, 1950s, McCoy mark. **$90-$110**

Left, **Village Smithy planter** in gold trim, 1950s, McCoy USA mark, 6 1/2" tall. Right, **Spinning wheel planter** with cat and dog, 1950s, McCoy mark, 7 1/4" tall. **$90-$110 each**

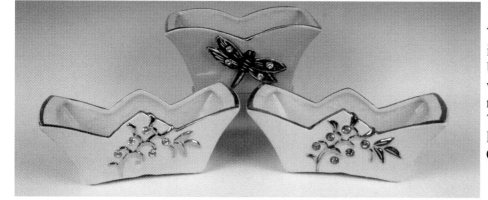

Three **Jeweled Line planters** in gold trim, 1950s, McCoy USA and Shafer marks, one with dragonfly, decorated with rhinestones (often missing), 7 1/2" and 8 1/2" wide. Dragonfly, **$150-$200;** Others, **$90-$110 each**

Left, **short Scroll planter,** 1950s, USA and Shafer marks, 4 1/2" tall. **$50-$60** Right, **Swan planter** in Sunburst glaze, 1950s, "USA McCoy 192 24K Gold" mark, also with atypical pink interior, 4 1/2" tall. **$100-$125**

Triple Pot planter in gold trim, 1950s, McCoy USA mark, 12 1/2" long. **$200-$225**

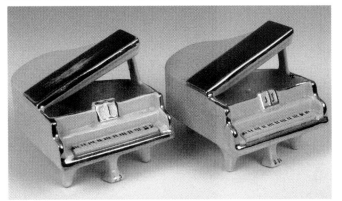

Two **Piano planters** in gold trim in white and yellow, late 1950s, McCoy USA mark, also found in matte black, 5" tall. **$300-$350 each**

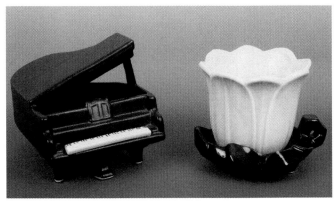

Left, **Piano planter** in matte black, late 1950s, McCoy USA mark, 5" tall. **$150-$175** Right, **Tulip planter** in pink and black, 1950s, McCoy USA mark, also found in green and gray, 4 1/2" tall. **$60-$70**

Left, **small fin planter,** early 1950s, USA McCoy mark, 3 1/2" tall. **$50-$60**
Right, **Trinket box** in unusual brocade glaze, 1960s, McCoy USA 464 mark, 3 1/2" tall. **$70-$80**

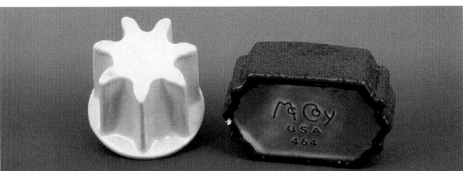

Two planters in gold trim. Left, **Rooster on Wheelbarrow,** mid-1950s, McCoy USA and Shafer marks, 7" tall. **$200-$225**
Right, **Lamb with Bells,** mid-1950s, McCoy mark, rare in gray, 7 1/2" tall. **$100-$125**

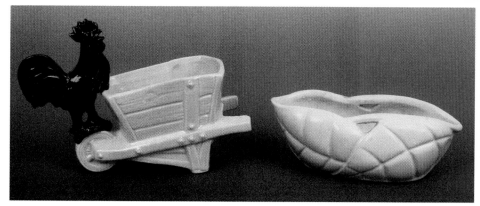

Left, **Rooster on Wheelbarrow planter** in black and yellow (rare colors), mid-1950s, McCoy USA mark, 7" tall. **$150-$170** in these colors
Right, **Leaf planter,** 1940s, McCoy mark, 9" long. **$50-$70**

Left, **Lotus leaf planter** in gold trim, 1950s, McCoy USA mark, 4 1/2" tall. **$50-$60**
Right, **Water Lily planter,** 1950s, McCoy USA mark, also found in green and rarely in orange, 3 1/2" tall. **$100-$125**

Triple Fawn planter in natural colors. **$250-$275**

Two **small Log planters** in gold trim, 1950s, McCoy and McCoy USA marks, 7" and 8 3/4" long. **$35-$45 each**

Triple Fawn planter in gold trim, 1950s, McCoy USA mark, 12" wide. **$400-$450** (Same price range for black and chartreuse glaze.)

Left, **Sand Butterfly planter** (also called a fern box) in gold trim, 1940s, McCoy USA mark, found in other pearly colors, 8 1/2" long. **$45-$55**
Right, **Scallop-edge planter** in gold trim, early 1960s, McCoy USA mark, 9" long. **$35-$45**

Planters

Ball planters in gold trim (also called rose bowl), 1940s, NM USA mark, 3 1/2" tall. **$45-$55** This form also comes in a 7" tall size with a McCoy mark. **$70-$80** in gold trim

Left, **Basket planter** in gold trim, 1950s, McCoy USA and Shafer mark, 9" wide. **$75-$90** Right, **Lotus form planter** (also called Brown Drip centerpiece) in gold trim, 1950s, McCoy mark, 9" wide. **$45-$55**

Left, **Centerpiece bowl/planter** with applied bird in gold trim, 1950s, McCoy mark, 10" wide. **$60-$75** Right, **Frog and Lotus planter,** late 1940s, unmarked, 4" tall. **$35-$45** (Beware of reproductions.)

Two **Stork planters** in gold trim, part of the Nursery Line, 1950s, McCoy USA and Shafer marks, rare in yellow, 7" tall. **$110-$125 each**

Two **Rocking Horse planters**, one in gold trim, one plain yellow (rare), part of the Nursery Line, 1950s, McCoy USA and Shafer mark. Gold trim, **$200-$225**; Yellow, **$225-$250** (in pink or green, **$125-$150**)

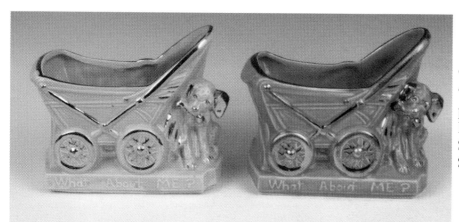

Two **Baby Buggy planters** (called "What About Me?") in gold trim, part of the Nursery Line, 1950s, McCoy USA mark, 6" tall. **$125-$150 each** (without gold trim, **$70-$80**).

Two **Cradle planters,** one in gold trim, one plain, part of the Nursery Line, 1950s, McCoy mark, 8 1/2" long. With gold trim, **$70-$80**; Plain, **$45-$55**

Two **Nursery Line planters.** Left, Dog with Cart, 1950s, McCoy USA mark, 8 1/2" long. **$45-$55** Right, Lamb with Bow, 1950s, McCoy USA mark, with cold paint, 8 1/2" long. **$45-$55,** depending on paint condition

 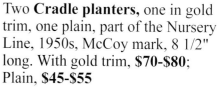

Planters

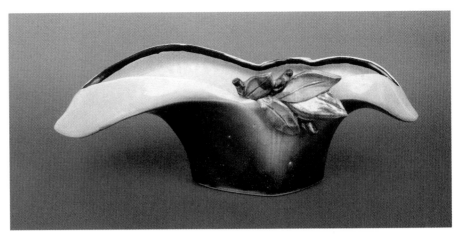

Fancy **Lily Bud planting dish,** late 1940s or early 50s, hand-painted under glaze, 11" long. **$85-$95**

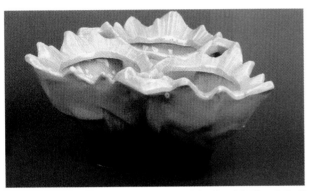

Triple bulb bowl in pink and black, 1950s, McCoy mark, 8" wide. **$165-$185**

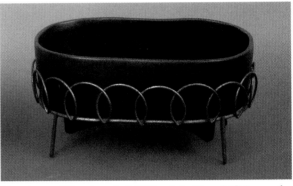

Planter with stand, 1950s, McCoy USA mark, 7" long. **$35-$45** with stand, which is often missing

Left, **Lotus planter** in gold trim, 1950s, McCoy USA mark, 4 1/2" tall. **$50-$60** Right, **Swimming duck planter** in gold trim, 1950s, McCoy USA mark. **$70-$80**

Left, **Swimming duck planter** with cold paint, 1950s, McCoy USA mark, 7" long. **$45-$55** Right, **Vine design planting dish** with hand-painted decoration under glaze, 1950s, McCoy USA mark, 8 1/2" long. **$60-$70**

Left, **planter,** came with metal stand, 1950s, McCoy USA mark. **$25-$35** with stand. Right, **planting dish,** 1940s, McCoy mark. **$35-$45**

Left, **Double Cornucopia planter** in gold trim, 1960s, McCoy may be visible, depending on glaze thickness. **$25-$30** Right, **Cup planter** with gold decoration, 1970s, McCoy LCC mark. **$10**

Left, **Stork planter** in green, part of the Nursery Line, 1950s, McCoy USA mark, 7" tall. **$110-$125** Right, **Snooty Poodle planter** (pierced base), 1950s, McCoy USA mark, also found in green and commonly in black, 7" tall. **$75-$90**

Four **Nursery Line planters,** all came with cold-paint decoration, 1950s, unmarked.
Left, Lamb with block, 4 1/2" tall. **$55-$65**; Baby scale, 5 1/2" tall. **$35-$45**; Rattle, 5 1/2" long. **$70-$80**; Raggedy Ann and blocks, 5 1/2" tall. **$75-$85** (prices vary depending on paint condition)

Left, **Snooty Poodle planter** (closed base, harder to find) in black with cold paint, McCoy USA mark, 7" tall. **$90-$110** Right, **Clown Riding a Pig planter** with cold paint, early 1950s, McCoy USA mark, 8 1/2" long. **$110-$125** (also found with pig having raised ears, rare)

Two **Cat with Basket planters** in glossy pink and yellow, early 1940s, NM USA mark, also found in white, 6" tall. **$50-$60 each**

Left, **Frog with Umbrella planter** in black (rare), mid-1950s, McCoy USA mark, with cold-paint decoration, 7 1/2" tall. **$150-$200** Right, **Carriage with Umbrella,** mid-1950s, McCoy USA mark, 9" tall. **$150-$200**

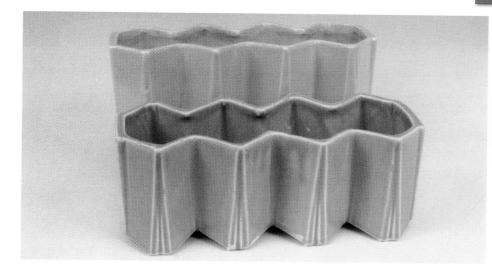

Two **jagged edge planters,** 1950s, McCoy USA mark, also found in yellow, 10" long. **$150-$200 each**

Left, **Boot and Football planter** in a non-production glaze, normally found in all brown with white or yellow cold paint, 1950s, McCoy USA mark, 4 1/4" tall. **$400-$450** as shown; Normally **$125-$175** Right, **Fence and Birds pot and saucer,** non-production piece, 1950s, McCoy USA mark, 4 1/2" tall. **$200-$250**

Large **Fish planter** in pink, green and white, 1950s, McCoy USA mark, 12" long. **$1,200+**

Planters

Three **Stretch Animal planters** (horse, butting goat, small lion), late 1930s to early '40s, unmarked, 3 1/4" to 4" tall. Horse, **$75-$90**; Goat, **$250-$300**; Lion, **$250-$300** (There are also a standing goat, a dachshund, angry dog, and larger lion in the Stretch Animals.)

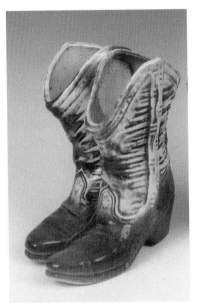

Cowboy boots planter (this form also used for lamp base), 1960s, McCoy USA mark, 7" tall. **$75-$85**

Small **Stretch Lion** in rare cobalt blue, 1940s, unmarked, 4" tall. **$250-$300**

Baa Baa Black Sheep planter, part of the Nursery Line, 1930s, NM USA mark, also found in yellow, blue, and white. **$50-$60**

Two **Wild Rose planters** in matte lavender and aqua, 1950s, McCoy mark. 4 1/2" tall, **$40-$45**; 6" tall, **$50-$60**

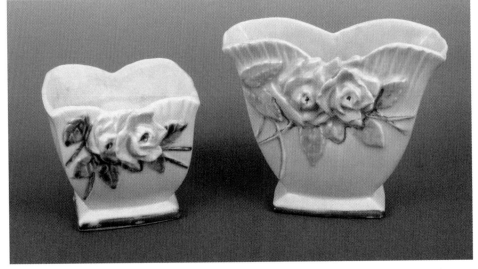

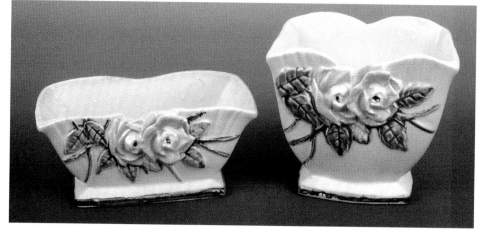

Two **Wild Rose planters** in matte yellow, 1950s, McCoy mark. 8 1/4" wide, **$60-$75; 6" tall, $45-$55**

Two **Dog with Blanket planters** (it's actually an Airedale holding a coat in its mouth, but nobody calls it that) in aqua and lavender, 1940s, NM USA mark, 5" tall. **$90-$110 each**

Two **Stretch Animal planters,** dachshund and large lion, in matte aqua, 1930s, unmarked. Dachshund, 8 1/2" long, **$150-$175;** Lion, 5 1/2" tall, **$350-$400**

Two **Lion planters** in matte aqua and "butterfly blue," 1940s, NM USA mark, also found in yellow and white, 8 1/4" long. **$110-$125 each**

Planters

Two **Nursery Line planters.** Left, **Rabbits and Stump** in yellow and blue (rare), also found in brown and yellow, and rustic ivory and brown, 1950s, McCoy USA mark, as shown. **$150-$175**
Right, **Lamb with Two Bells planter** in rare gray, 1950s, McCoy mark, 7 1/2" tall. **$125-$150**

Zigzag planting dish in matte aqua, 1940s, NM USA mark, 9 1/2" long. **$110-$125**

Two **figural planters** in matte aqua. Left, Rooster, 1940s, NM mark, 6" tall. **$60-$70** Right, Pelican, 1940s, NM mark, 7 1/2" long. **$45-$50**

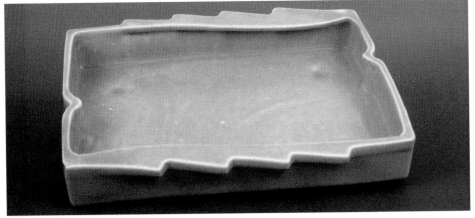

Two **Pony planters** in matte aqua and yellow, 1940s, NM USA mark, 5" tall. **$80-$90 each**

Two **Deer planters** in matte aqua. Left, doe and fawn, 1940s, NM USA mark or unmarked (reissued in the 1950s in glossy yellow and green), 7" tall. **$60-$70** Right, backwards deer (one of the "ladder pieces," so named because they were pictured in an early McCoy guide on a drying rack that was tiered like the steps of a ladder), 1940s, NM mark, 4 1/2" tall. **$80-$90**

Left, **Stump planter** with rare "Ted & Anne" theme, 1950s, McCoy mark, also found in yellow and green, 4" tall. **$60-$70** Right, **Swans planter** in green, 1950s, McCoy mark, common in white and yellow, 8 1/2" long. In green, **$30-$40**

Left, **Stump planter** with more common "ST-VH" initials in glossy green, 1950s, McCoy mark, also found in yellow and green, 4" tall. **$25-$35** Right, **Ducks and eggs planter** in purple glaze (rare color), 1950s, McCoy USA mark, 5" tall. **$55-$65** in this color; Otherwise, **$30-$40**

Planters

Two **Petal basket planters** (uncommon in darker glazes at left), 1950s, McCoy USA mark, 8 3/4" tall. Darker, **$110-$125;** Lighter, **$75-$90**

Swan planting dish in rustic ivory and turquoise, 1950s, McCoy USA mark, 8 1/2" tall. **$700-$800**

Swan planting dish in chartreuse and black, 1950s, McCoy USA mark, 8 1/2" tall. **$700-$800**

Left, **Swimming Swan planter** with under-glaze decoration, 1950s, McCoy mark, 7" tall. **$40-$50** Right, **Harmony planting dish,** 1960s, McCoy USA mark, 8 1/2" long. **$20-$25**

Left, **Pheasant planter,** 1950s, McCoy USA mark, 6" tall. **$70-$80** Right, **Puppy planter,** late 1950s, McCoy USA mark, 6" tall. **$50-$60**

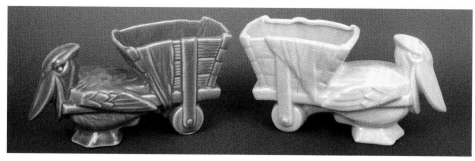

Two **Pelican and Cart planters** in glossy aqua and yellow, 1940s, NM mark, 4 1/2" tall. **$55-$65 each**

Two **Cornucopia planters** in glossy aqua and yellow, 1940s, NM USA mark, also found in white, 5" tall. **$30-$35 each**

Two **"S" planting dishes** in matte white (tripod feet) and glossy aqua (four curving line feet), 1940s, NM USA mark, note that white dish is slightly shallower, 8" long. **$25-$30 each**

Planters

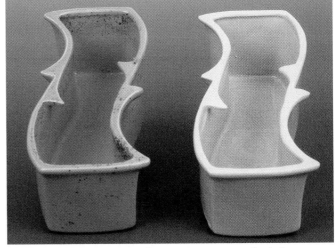

Two **Bear and Ball planters,** part of the Nursery line, late 1940 or early 50s, with cold paint, McCoy USA mark, 5 1/2" tall. **$125-$150 each**

Two **Spiked planters** in matte aqua and pink, 1950s, McCoy USA mark, 9" long. **$50-$60 each**

Left, **Ivy planter,** 1950s, McCoy USA mark, 3" tall. **$30-$40** Center, **planting dish,** 1940s, NM USA mark, 9" long. **$35-$45** Right, small **Cornucopia planter,** 1950s, unmarked, 4 1/2" tall. **$35-$45**

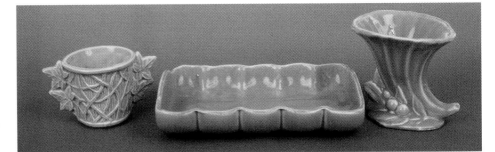

Round planting dish in matte aqua, late 1940s, McCoy mark, 8 1/4" diameter. **$35-$45**

Two small **Trough planters** in glossy white and aqua, late 1950s, USA mark, 6" wide. **$20-$25 each**

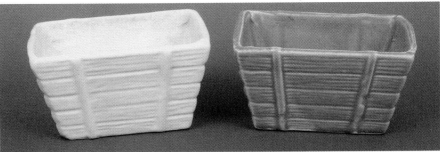

Two **Bird Dog planters,** late 1950s, McCoy USA mark, one with speckled glaze, 7 3/4" long. **$125-$150 each**

Pedestal Line window box or planting dish, 1959, McCoy USA mark, 11" wide. **$35-$40**

Cat with Bow planter with cold paint decoration, 1950s, McCoy USA mark on back, 7" long. **$40-$50**

Large **Turtle planter** in dark green and pink, 1950s, McCoy USA mark, 12 1/2" long. **$175-$225**

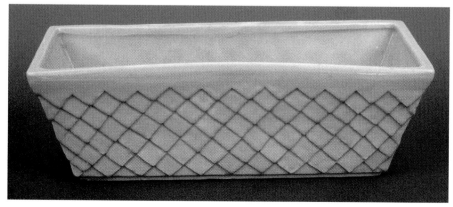

Window box in glossy pink, 1950s, McCoy mark, 10" wide. **$25-$30**

Elephant planter in matte aqua, attributed to McCoy, unmarked, 9" tall, with attribution. **$100**

Two **Wishing Well planters,** late 1940s to early '50s, McCoy USA mark, gray and turquoise glaze is harder to find. 6" tall, **$25-$35;** Larger (7") size, **$55-$65**

Two **Lamb planters** in glossy black and gray, 1940s, NM USA mark, 3" tall. **$55-$65 each**

Large **Centerpiece planter,** 1950s, McCoy USA mark, found in other colors, 12" long. **$90-$110**

Auto planter, 1950s, unmarked, 6" tall. **$45-$55**

Two **Crestwood pieces.** Left, Pedestal planter, 12" tall. Right, Boat planter, 13" long, mid-1960s, McCoy USA with original labels. **$60-$70 each**

Grecian Line window box, 1950s, McCoy USA mark with style number 435, 12" long. **$85-$95**

Large **Leaf planter** in matte green, 1930s, stoneware, unmarked, 6 1/2" tall. **$80-$90** (This form was reissued in the 1950s as part of the Garden Club Line).

Grecian Line pedestal planter, 1950s, McCoy USA mark with style number 442, 8" wide. **$50-$60**

Rustic Line planter with seven wide-eyed animal faces (probably intended to be fawns) peering out of the foliage, called by some collectors "the devil dog planter" or "gremlins planter," 1940s, McCoy mark, 6" tall. **$60-$70**

Planters

Left, **Icicles window box,** 1950s, McCoy USA mark, 8 1/2" long. **$70-$80**
Right, **Garden Club pedestal planter,** late 1950s, McCoy USA mark, 7" tall. **$40-$50**

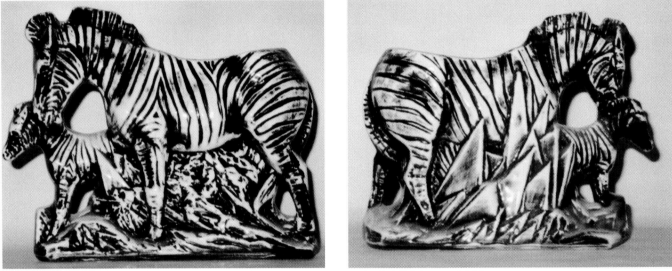

Two views of the **Zebra planter,** 1950s, McCoy USA mark, 8 1/2" long. **$800+**

Oak Leaf and Acorn basket in matte white, early 1950s, McCoy USA mark. **$60-$70**

Parrot planter in matte white, 1940s, NM mark, 7 1/2" tall. **$70-$80**

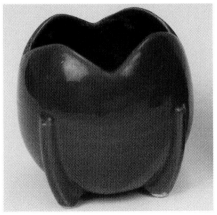

Ball planter (also called rose bowl), 1940s, NM mark. 3 1/2" tall, **$35-$45** (This form also comes in a 7" tall size with a McCoy mark, **$60-$70**.) The shorter size was a popular choice for glaze tests and may be found with inscribed glaze numbers.

Basket planter hand-painted by Leslie Cope, signed, 7" tall. **$700-$1,000**

Small planter usually found in pink or blue, with under-glaze decoration, 1940s, 5" tall. **$45-$55**

Old Mill planter, in gold trim, 1950s, McCoy USA mark, 6 1/2" tall. **$90-$110**

Large **Fish planter,** found in other colors, 1950s, McCoy mark, 12" long. **$1,200-$1,400**

Small **Cornucopia planter** in gold trim, 1950s, McCoy mark, 4" tall. **$40-$50**

Leaves and Berries hanging basket planter in matte green, 1930s, unmarked, 5 1/4" diameter. **$60-$70**

Butterfly hanging basket planter in non-production dark green glaze, early 1940s, NM mark. As shown, **$500-$600**; In pastel colors, **$225-$250**

Leaves and Berries hanging basket planter in matte aqua, 1930s, unmarked, 6" tall. **$50-$60**

Water Lily planter with green and tan details, normally found in all green and yellow, 1950s, unmarked, 7 1/4" long. **$50-$60**

Antique Curio

Planters, Vases, Jardinieres styled in an Early American theme
AVAILABLE IN
Matt White, Gloss Green, Gloss Brown w/Decorated Grape Pattern

McCoy U.S.A.

1609 7″

1605 7″

1604 10″

1607 14″

1603 6″

1604 10″

1601 5″

1609 7″

1602 7″

1608 7½″

1605 7″

1606 10″

1602 7″

THE NELSON McCOY POTTERY COMPANY
Factory - Office   Roseville, Ohio

The Antique Curio line featured planters, vases, and jardinières styled in an early American theme.

SILHOUETTE

Satin Glazed Planters

Our Golden Anniversary line featuring new shapes in satin glazes of white, green, turquoise, yellow, and brown. Available in a 22K brushed gold decoration or plain finish.

GI104 - 12"

GI101 - 6"

1107 - 6½"

1104 - 12"

GI108 - 8"

1103 - 10¼"

1101 - 6"

GI107 - 6½"

GI103 - 10¼"

GI106 - 7"

1109B - 10"

1106 - 7"

1108 - 8"

1105 - 7½"   GI105 - 7½"

THE NELSON McCOY POTTERY COMPANY

Factory - Office   **Roseville, Ohio**

Printed in U.S.A.

LITHOGRAPHY BY PAPPAS BROS. PARKERSBURG, W. VA.

The Silhouette line of satin glazed planters came out when McCoy was celebrating its Golden Anniversary.

31-1638-01
5½"
Aztec Pot & Saucer
Hanging Planter

31-1644-77
9½" Pot & Saucer
Hanging Planter,

31-1623-46
6½" x 8½"
Double Woven Hanging
Planter Baskets,

31-1625-01
Tub Hanging Planter,
6½"h x 9"w,
Assorted colors—
OFF SELECTION,
Limited quantity—
Not available for listings.

31-1618-87
Owl Hanging Planter,
7¾"h x 7¼"w,

31-1624-77
5½" x 7½" Double Pot
and Saucer Hanging
Planter,

1975

31-1625-01
Tub Hanging Planter,
6½"h x 9"w,
Assorted colors—
OFF SELECTION,
Limited quantity—
Not available for listings.

31-1620-85
Birdie Hanging Planter
(Planting area 4½" deep)
7"h x 12"w,

31-1639-01
7½" Aztec Pot & Saucer
Hanging Planter

31-1621-84
Fish Hanging Planter,
5½"h x 11"w,

31-1619-46
Owl Hanging Planter
7¾"h x 7¼"w,

31-0771-77
9½" Pot & Saucer,

31-3023-46
8½" Jardiniere Basket
Weave,

More than a dozen versions of hanging planters were displayed in McCoy groupings.

Planters

The Starburst Line

No. 11

No. 14

No. 13

No. 20

No. 16

No. 20

No. 15

No. 12

No. 17

No. 20

The Nelson McCoy Pottery Company
Subsidiary of Mount Clemens Pottery Company
Area Code 614-697-3331   Roseville, Ohio 43777

The Starburst Line included flowerpots, planters, and vases.

The Nelson McCoy Pottery Company
Roseville, Ohio

1964

Tonecraft

High quality planters and flower bowls with
eye appeal plus

All items available in four basic colors as shown —
Hand decorated with rich copper and gold metallic
tones: Frosted White, Nile Green, Oriental Orange,
Copper Black.

M1 — Low Pedestal Dish

M2 — Square Pedestal Planter

M3 — Oval Pedestal Planter

M4 — Round Flower Bowl

M5 — Footed Planter

M6 — Pedestal Jardiniere

M7 — Scalloped Flower Bowl

M8 — Rectangle Planter

M9 — Jardiniere

M10 — Oblong Pedestal Planter

The Tonecraft line of planters and flower pots had "eye appeal plus," according to McCoy.

ANTIQUE ROSE LINE

Flower Bowls, Planters, Vases Designed For An Antique Look

Available in two colors—Pure white or two-tone brown and flecked blue—Decorated in an old fashioned moss rose pattern and trimmed in bright gold.

   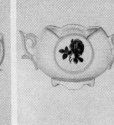 

No. 370—7 x 6" Sprinkling Can Planter White or Two-tone Brown and Flecked Blue. Red Rose Decoration. GOLD Trim Pkd. 1 Doz. Wt. 16 lbs. $21.20 per Doz.	No. 371—7½ x 5½" Swan Planter White or Two-tone Brown and Flecked Blue. Red Rose Decoration. GOLD Trim Pkd. ½ Doz. Wt. 12 lbs. $28.30 per Doz.	No. 372—9" Pitcher Vase White or Two-tone Brown and Flecked Blue. Red Rose Decoration. GOLD Trim Pkd. ½ Doz. Wt. 10 lbs. $28.30 per Doz.	No. 373—9½ x 6½" Flower Bowl White or Two-tone Brown and Flecked Blue. Red Rose Decoration. GOLD Trim Pkd. ½ Doz. Wt. 15 lbs. $33.40 per Doz.	No. 374—12 x 7½" Low Flower Bowl White or Two-tone Brown and Flecked Blue. Red Rose Decoration. GOLD Trim Pkd. 1/3 Doz. Wt. 14 lbs. $42.60 per Doz.

Order Open Stock or in the Following 12 Pc. Trial Assortment
No. 95068—12 Pc. "ANTIQUE ROSE" Planter-Vase Assortment
Consisting of:
4 Only No. 370   2 Each Nos. 372; 373
3 Only No. 371   1 Only No. 374
Pkd. 1 Carton—Wt. 25 lbs. $28.00 per Assortment

Pedestal Line

Contemporary styling on a group of planter bowls, planting dishes, jardinieres and vases in green, white, yellow and pink gloss glazes with a decorated bisque foot.

No. 802—Pedestal Jardiniere Sizes 7"-9" Green, Pink, Yellow or White w/Decorated Foot 7"—$14.40 per Doz. 1 Doz. 26 lbs. 8"—$24.60 per Doz. ½ Doz. 26 lbs.	No. 803—Pedestal Planter Bowl Sizes 5"-6" Green, Yellow or Pink w/Decorated Foot 5"—$ 8.80 per Doz. 2 Doz. 22 lbs. 6"—$10.40 per Doz. 1 Doz. 19 lbs.	No. 804—6½" Hanging Basket w/Cord Green, Yellow or Pink w/Decorated Foot Pkd. 1 Doz. Wt. 14 lbs. $14.40 per Doz.	No. 805—Pedestal Planting Dish Sizes 7"-11" Green, Yellow or Pink w/Decorated Foot 7"—$ 9.70 per Doz. 2 Doz. 28 lbs. 11"—$17.60 per Doz. 1 Doz. 28 lbs.

No. 806—8" Low Centerpiece Green, Yellow or White w/Decorated Foot Pkd. 1 Doz. Wt. 22 lbs. $14.40 per Doz.	No. 807—Vase Sizes 8"-10" Green, Pink, Yellow or White w/Decorated Foot 8"—$14.40 per Doz. 1 Doz. 23 lbs. 11"—$24.60 per Doz. ½ Doz. 25 lbs.

Order Open Stock or From the Following 72 Pc. Assortment
No. 2968—72 Pc. "PEDESTAL LINE" Assortment
Consisting of:
8 Only No. 802—7"
4 Only No. 802—9"
8 Each Nos. 803—5"; 803—6"; 804; 805—7"; 805—11"; 806; 807—8"
4 Only No. 807—10"
Pkd. 4 Cartons—Wt. 145 lbs.
$86.00 per Assortment

The Nelson-McCoy Pottery Company . . . Roseville, Ohio

A variety of planters, flower bowls, and vases were included in the Antique Rose line from McCoy.

INDOOR-OUTDOOR HANGING PLANTERS

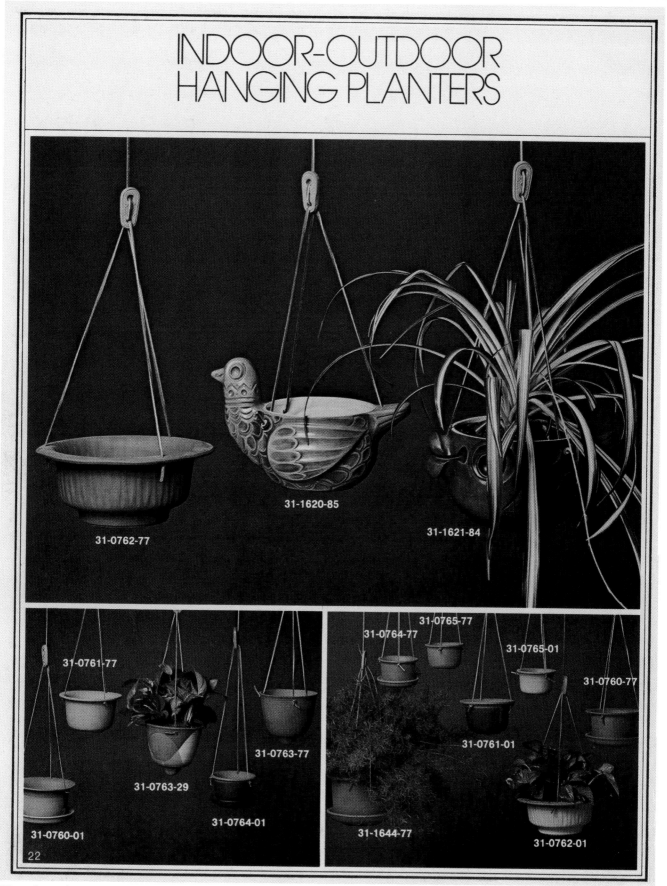

31-0762-77

31-1620-85

31-1621-84

31-0761-77

31-0763-29

31-0760-01

31-0763-77

31-0764-01

31-0764-77

31-0765-77

31-0765-01

31-0760-77

31-0761-01

31-1644-77

31-0762-01

22

Hanging planters were the theme of this spread in a 1976 McCoy catalog.

McCoy Pottery sign, contemporary, by Billie and Nelson McCoy, signed and dated 2001, 4 1/2" by 8 1/2". **$40-$50**

Two **McCoy Pottery signs.** Left: sign intended for use at JC Penney stores, 4" by 5 1/4". **$400-$450**
Right: contemporary sign by Billie and Nelson McCoy, 4" by 5 1/4". **$250-$300**

Block used to make the mold for "The Pottery Shop by McCoy" signs. **$1000**

Vases & Flower Holders

Second only to planters in their variety, vases also present special challenges, because many of them lack formal names. Collectors use descriptions like "the vase with the low drape handles" or "the one that looks like a chevron." Others define collecting areas based on glazes (matte aqua or the glossy palette) and seek examples in the smaller sizes.

Two **Arrow Leaf vases** in matte aqua and coral, 1940s, McCoy mark or unmarked, 7 1/2" tall. **$85-$95 each**

Two **Butterfly Line "V" vases** in matte blue and yellow, 1940s, NM USA mark, 9" tall. **$90-$110**

Three **Butterfly Line vases** in matte blue, yellow, and white. Left, cylinder vase, 1940s, NM USA or NM mark, 8" tall. **$75-$85**
Center, two-handled vase, 1940s, USA mark, 10" tall. **$200-$225**
Right, cylinder vase, NM mark, 6" tall. **$55-$65**

Two **Butterfly Line cylinder vases** in matte white and yellow, 1940s, NM USA mark, 8" tall. **$75-$85 each**

Antique Rose low flower bowl in blue with transfer decoration, 1959, McCoy USA mark, 12" wide. **$55-$65** Also found in white with red or brown rose.

Two **Antique Rose pieces** in blue with transfer decoration. Flower bowl, 9 1/2" wide, and pitcher vase, 9" tall, 1959, McCoy USA mark. **$45-$55 each** Also found in white with red or brown rose.

Tassel vase in glossy raspberry, 1930s, stoneware, unmarked, 8" tall. **$75-$85**

Wheat vase 1950s, McCoy USA mark, 8" tall. **$55-$65**

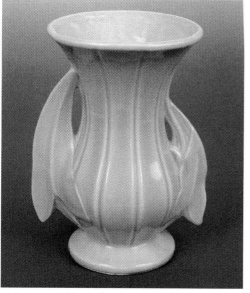

Vase in glossy yellow (rare, sometimes called an Arrow Leaf but different from other vases in that form), 1950s, McCoy mark, 8" tall. **$550-$600**

Two **vases** in matte coral and aqua, one faceted, one smooth, 1940s, NM mark, 9" tall. **$55-$65 each**

Two **vases** in glossy coral and yellow, 1950s, McCoy mark, 9" tall. **$60-$70 each**

Two **vases** in glossy white, late 1950s, unmarked, 8 1/2" and 8 1/4" tall. Left with transfer decoration of roses, **$45-$55;** Right, **$65-$75**

Vases and Flower Holders

Leaves and Berries vase in matte brown and green, unmarked, 7" tall. **$80-$90**

Two **Hand vases** in matte aqua, 1940s, NM USA mark. 7 1/2" tall, **$125-$150**; 5" tall, **$55-$65**

Three small **flower holders** in glossy white, pink, and yellow, 1930s, NM mark or unmarked, 3 1/4" tall. **$60-$70 each** McCoy matte colors include aqua, blue, lavender, white, yellow, and brown and green.

Vase in matte brown and green, 12" tall. **$150-$175**

Blossomtime vases in yellow, 1940s, McCoy mark, one matte, one glossy. 6 3/4" tall, **$70-$80**; 8" tall, **$60-$70**

Pink Poppy vases showing variations in glaze intensity, McCoy mark, 8 1/2" wide. **$350-$450 each** (see other colors on p.224)

Heart vase in matte white, unmarked, 6" tall, and spherical **Leaves and Berries vase,** unmarked, 6 1/2" tall. **$60-$70 each**

Blossomtime vases in matte white, 1940s, McCoy mark. 6 3/4" tall, **$70-$80**; 8" tall, **$60-$70**

Two **Blossomtime vases,** 1940s, McCoy mark, 6 1/2" tall. **$50-$60 each**

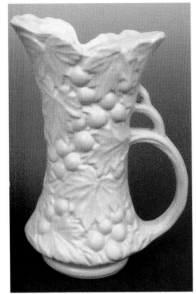

Grape pitcher vase in matte white, 9" tall, early 1950s, McCoy mark. **$50-$60**

Two **Hourglass vases** in matte yellow and pink, 1930s, unmarked, 8" tall. **$90-$110 each**

Four **Stoneware Hourglass vases** in matte white, unmarked, 1930s, also found in varying shades of green, and brown and green. Note variations in mold crispness.
5" tall, **$50-$60;**
10" tall, **$100-$125**;
14" tall, **$225-$250**

Three **Stoneware Hourglass vases** in matte white, 1930s, unmarked, also found in yellow, pink, varying shades of green, and brown and green.
12" tall, **$200-$225**;
8" tall, **$90-$110**;
6" tall, **$75-$90**

Left, **Hourglass vase** in matte green glaze, 1930s, stoneware, unmarked, 14" tall. **$400-$450**
Right, **Stoneware Urn vase** in glossy green glaze, hard-to-find form, 1930s, unmarked, 8" tall. **$250-$275**

Left, **Cat vase** in matte black (also found in white and gray), 1960s, McCoy USA, 14" tall. **$225-$250**
Right, **Antique Curio Line vase** in glossy brown (also found in green and white), 1960s, McCoy USA mark, 14 1/2" tall. **$110-$125**

Three **Blossomtime vases**, mid-1940s, McCoy mark. **$100-$150 each** because of atypical flower and leaf glaze colors. Normally **$50-$60 each** in white or yellow with pink flowers.

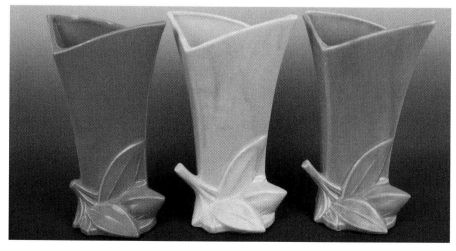

Three **Lily Bud vases** in matte blue, lavender, and aqua, 1940s, NM USA mark (also found unmarked), 10" tall. **$125-$150 each** (Note short stem on blue vase, not a break, as it came from the factory.)

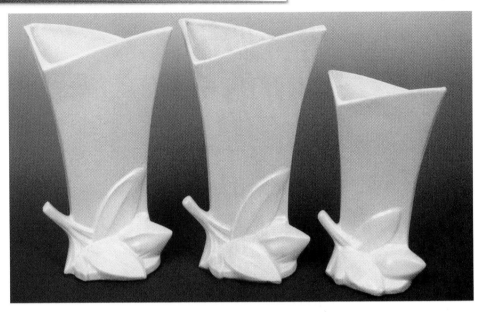

Three **Lily Bud vases** in matte white and yellow, 1940s, NM USA mark (also found unmarked).
8" tall, **$80-$90 each;**
10" tall, **$125-$150 each**

Three **Leaves and Berries vases** with tab or ear handles in matte white, 1930s, unmarked.
5" tall, **$80-$90**;
8" tall, **$90-$110**

Three tall **Cornucopia vases** in matte white, 1930s, unmarked.
5" tall, **$75-$100**;
8" tall, **$50-$75**;
10" tall, **$100-$125**

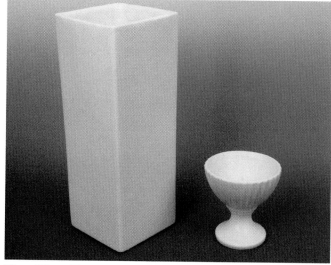

Two **Floraline vases** in matte white, 1960s, both marked Floraline USA. 10" rectangular vase, **$45-$55**; 3 1/2" chalice, **$15-$20**

Square Cherry vase, stoneware, 1930s, unmarked. **$100-$125**

Left, **Leafy vase** in matte white, 1940s, unmarked, 7 1/2" tall. **$100-$125** Center and right, two **Arrow Leaf vases** in matte white, 1940s, unmarked. 10" tall, **$125-$150**; 8" tall, **$90-$110**

Ram's Head vase in matte white (rare, usually chartreuse, black, or burgundy), 1950s, McCoy mark, 9 1/2" tall. **$250-$300** (in other colors, **$100-$125**)

Two **Baluster vases** in matte white, 1940s, unmarked, heights vary from 12" to almost 13". With handles, **$150-$175**; Without handles, **$200-$250**

Vases and Flower Holders

From left: **Lily Bud pin dish**, NM mark, 5 1/2" wide. **$40-$50** **Miniature oil jar**, 4 1/4" tall. **$40-$50**. **Small Hand vase** (fingers separated), 6 1/2" tall. **$100-$125** **Fish flower holder** (one of the "ladder pieces," so named because they were pictured in an early McCoy guide on a drying rack that was tiered like the steps of a ladder), 1940s to 1950s, 3 1/4" tall. **$90-$125,** depending on color

Three **Fish flower holders** (one of the "ladder pieces," so named because they were pictured in an early McCoy guide on a drying rack that was tiered like the steps of a ladder), 1940s, NM USA mark, 3 1/4" tall. **$90-$125,** depending on color

Two **matte white vases,** one with leaves (Stoneware, late 1920s), one with loop handles, 1930s, unmarked. 12" tall, **$200-$250**; 10" tall, **$100-$125**

Left, **Fin or Ribbed vase** in matte white, 14" tall, unmarked. **$250-$300** Right, **Fin or Ribbed planter** in matte white, 7" tall, unmarked (may also be found with saucer base). **$90-$110**

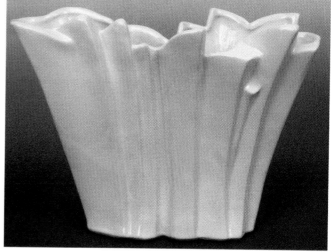

Miniature Turtle flower holder (one of the "ladder pieces," so named because they were pictured in a early McCoy guide on a drying rack that was tiered like the steps of a ladder), 1940s to 1950s, NM mark, 4" long. **$80-$100 Miniature Vase flower holder,** NM mark, 3" tall. **$55-$65**

Large Fan vase, also called "Blades of Grass," glossy white (also found in green and black), late 1950s, McCoy USA mark, 10" tall. **$175-$225**

Three 9" **matte white vases,** from left: two-handled vase, 1930s, McCoy mark; **large Swan vase,** 1950s (generally, colored glazes were earlier, mid-1940s); **Sailboat vase** (seen here with round bottom, sailboat motif also found on narrower vase with square bottom). **$70-$90 each**

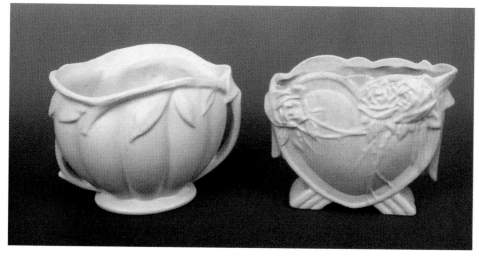

Left, **Lily Bud pillow vase** in matte white, 1940s, NM mark. Right, **Heart vase** in matte white, 1940s, unmarked, each 6" tall. **$60-$70 each**

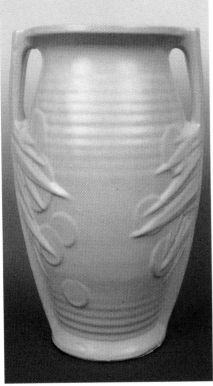

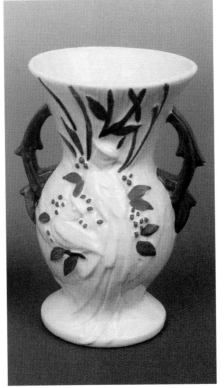

Sand Dollar vase in matte white, stoneware, 1940s, unmarked, also found in pastel colors, and brown and green. **$250-$300,** depending on color

Bird of Paradise vase with cold paint decoration (not factory), found in glossy colors, late 1940s, unmarked, 8 1/4" tall. **$40-$50**

Butterfly cylinder vase with under-glaze decoration, 1940s, NM mark, 8" tall. **$350-$450** (in typical colors of coral, yellow, blue, or green, **$60-$90**)

Two **Drape-handle vases** in matte white, 1940s, unmarked, also found in 6", 8", and 10" sizes, and glossy green, blue, and yellow. 12" tall, **$90-$110**; 9" tall, **$60-$75**

Hyacinth vases in a range of glazes, early 1950s, McCoy mark, 8" tall. **$150-$225 each,** depending on glaze intensity and mold crispness

Two **Magnolia vases,** left example having the more typical glaze combination, early 1950s, McCoy mark, 8 1/2" tall. **$250-$300 each**

Tall Double Tulip vases in a range of glazes, late 1940s, McCoy mark, 8" tall. **$100-$125 each**

Low Double Tulip vases, with right example having the more typical glaze, early 1950s, McCoy mark, 6 1/2" tall. **$225-$250 each**

Two Poppy vases in pink and yellow (harder to find), mid-1950s, McCoy mark. **$800-$1,000 each,** depending on glaze intensity and mold crispness

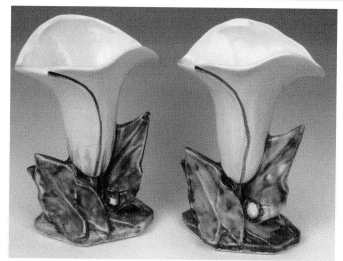

Single Lily bud vases, usually white or yellow with decoration under glaze, late 1940s, McCoy mark, 8" tall. **$90-$110 each**

Two **Wild Rose vases** with atypical glaze combinations, usually blue, lavender, pink, and yellow (with pink flowers), early 1950s, McCoy mark. In these colors, **$175-$200 each**; In common colors, **$80-$100 each**

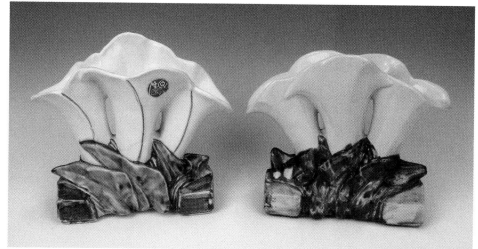

Triple Lily vases, one with original paper label, seen in matte white (front) and glossy yellow (back), also comes in glossy white, early 1950s, McCoy mark, 8 1/2" tall. **$100-$125 each**

Two **Chrysanthemum vases** in typical glazes, early 1950s, McCoy mark, 8 1/4" tall. **$150-$200 each,** depending on glaze intensity and mold crispness

Two **Chrysanthemum vases** in atypical glazes, early 1950s, McCoy mark, 8 1/4" tall. Left, **$150-$200**. Right, **$275-$300**

Vases and Flower Holders

Two **Large Lily vases** in typical glazes (blue leaves are matte, green are glossy), mid-1950s, McCoy mark, 8 1/2" tall. **$500-$600 each**

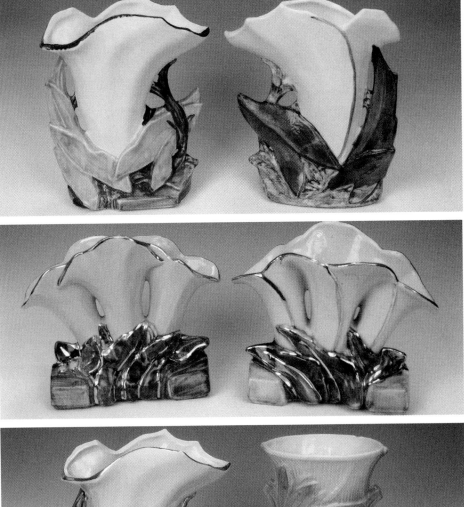

Triple Lily vases with gold trim, early 1950s, McCoy mark, 8 1/2" tall. **$125-$150 each**

Left, **large Lily vase** in gold trim, mid-1950s, McCoy mark, 8 1/2" tall. **$700-$800** Right, rare **Tulip vase** in air-brush decoration, 1950s, McCoy mark, 8 1/4" tall. **$800-$1,000**

Left, **Low Double Tulip vase** in gold trim, early 1950s, McCoy USA mark, 6 1/2" tall. **$325-$375** Right, **Magnolia vase** in gold trim, early 1950s, McCoy mark, 8 1/2" tall. **$350-$400**

Three **Leaves and Berries fan vases,** commonly found in aqua, pink, white and yellow; cobalt blue is hard to find, and the under-glaze decorated example at left is very rare; late 1930s or early 40s, McCoy USA or unmarked, 6" tall. Left, **$175-$200**; Center, **$110-$125**; Right, **$75-$90** (Beware of reproductions, which are lighter, have soft mold details, and thinner glazes.)

Two **Leaves and Berries fan vases** in white and burgundy, 1940s, burgundy with round McCoy USA mark, white with McCoy USA mark, 6" tall. **$70-$90 each**

Two **Hourglass vases**, Stoneware, 1930s, unmarked, 5" tall (a hard-to-find size). **$70-$90 each**

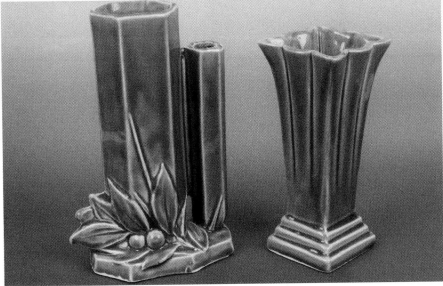

Left, **Double Bud vase,** 1940s, McCoy or unmarked, also found in aqua, cobalt blue, turquoise, and yellow, 8" tall. **$75-$90** Right, **Stepped-Base vase,** 1940s, round McCoy USA mark, 7" tall. **$40-$45**

Vase once thought to be Shawnee but later found in a McCoy catalog page, late 1940s, unmarked, 6 1/2" tall. **$35-$45**

Three vases in blue. Left, **Double Bud vase** in glossy cobalt, 1940s, NM mark, also found in aqua, dark green, turquoise, and yellow. **$75-$90** Center, **Stoneware vase** in blue with "flat flower," 1930s, unmarked, 7" tall. **$175-$200** Right, **two-handled vase** in cobalt, 1950s, unmarked, 7" tall. **$40-$50**

Left, **"V" vase** in glossy green glaze, mid-1920s, V2 mark, this style also found without handles, 9" tall. **$90-$110** Right, **"Number 50" vase** in glossy burgundy, 1930s, unmarked, 9" tall. **$100-$125**

Two **Leaves and Berries vases** (sometimes called the stovepipe), 1930s, unmarked, in what McCoy called "onyx" glazes, 8" tall. **$80-$90 each**

Ivy vase (also called English Ivy) in an atypical maroon and yellow, hand-painted, (normally white or yellow), 1950s, McCoy mark, 9" tall. As shown, **$800+;** Normally, **$125-$150**

Ring ware vase, 1920s, unmarked, 9 1/4" tall. **$100-$125**

Vase with low drape handles in glossy blue glaze, 1940s, unmarked, 10" tall. **$80-$90**

Left, **two-handled vase** with post-factory decoration, 1940s, NM mark (reproductions found with McCoy mark), 9" tall. **$40-$45** Right, **Lizard handle vase** in matte white with post-factory decoration, mid- to late-1930s, unmarked, 9" tall (also comes in 10"). **$200-$225** (also found in green and brown)

Left, **Blossomtime vase** in atypical glaze (white flower), mid-1940s, McCoy mark, 8" tall. **$100-$150** Right, non-production vase with applied berries and leaves, hand cut from a taller vase, ex-Cope Collection, 5" tall. **No established value.**

Leaves and Berries urn-form vase in matte white with small handles and unusual interior ring pattern, hard to find form, stoneware, 1930s, 8" tall. **$300-$350**

Non-production vase in a variation on the Blossomtime form, with applied flowers and decorated under glaze, mid-1940s, 8" tall. **No established value.**

Tall Fan vase in atypical glossy white (normally found in chartreuse and green, or yellow and maroon), mid-1950s, McCoy mark, 15" tall, also found in 10" As shown, **$350-$400**; Same size, other colors, **$150-$200**; 10" size, **$75-$90**

Large Swan vase and **two-handled vase**, both in gold trim, 1950s to 1960s, McCoy USA, 9" tall. **$90-$100 each**

Fawn vase and **Chicken pitcher vase** (also with floral decal) in gold trim, 1950s, McCoy and McCoy USA mark. Fawn vase 9" tall, **$125-$150**; Chicken, **$90-$110**

Two **vases** in glossy yellow and pink with gold trim, 1950s, McCoy USA and Shafer marks, also found in blue and white, 9" tall. **$90-$110 each**

Two **vases** in gold trim. Left, Ivy motif (also called English Ivy), 1950s, McCoy USA mark, 9" tall. **$150-$175** Right, Tulip motif, 1950s, USA mark, also with hand-applied inscription, "M.W. Rosendahl, 1955," 8" tall. **$100-$125**

Left, **Low Double Tulip vase** in gold trim, early 1950s, McCoy USA mark, 6 1/2" tall. Right, **Triple Lily vase** with gold trim, early 1950s, McCoy mark, 8 1/2" tall. **$175-$225**

Two **gold trim vases**. Left, Magnolia, 1950s, McCoy USA mark, 7 1/2" tall. **$250-$300** Right, Hyacinth, 1950s, McCoy USA mark, slightly duller gold finish, probably by McCoy, not Shafer, 8" tall. **$400-$425**

Two **presentation vases** in gold trim. Left, Tulip motif, 1950s, McCoy mark, also with hand-applied inscription, "50 Golden Years" and signed E.P. Aurand, 8" tall. Right, McCoy mark, with hand-applied inscription, "1949 Iowa State Glad Show, Waterloo," signed E.P.A., 9" tall. **$125-$150 each**

Two **gold trim vases**. Left, Sunflower, 1950s, unmarked, 9" tall. Right, ewer with hand-painted grapes under glaze, late 1940s, initialed W, 9" tall. **$150-$175 each**

Poppy vase in gold trim, 1950s, McCoy mark, reverse not gold trimmed, 8 1/2" wide. **$1,000-$1,200**

Two **gold trim vases**. Left, Bird and Berries, 1950s, McCoy USA mark, 8" tall. **$125-$150** Right, Petal vase (also called Celery vase), 1950s, McCoy USA mark, 9" tall. **$250-$300**

Three **miniature flower holders** in Sunburst gold (the Cornucopia and Swan are "ladder pieces," so named because they were pictured in a early McCoy guide on a drying rack that was tiered like the steps of a ladder), 1940s to 1950s, unmarked, 3 1/4" tall. **$60-$70,** depending on color

Two **Ripple Ware vases** in gold trim, glossy yellow and turquoise, early 1950s, McCoy mark, also found in other colors with dripping glazed rims, 7" tall. **$90-$110 each**

Left, **Grape vase** in gold trim, 1950s, McCoy USA mark, also found with brown and green glazes, 9" tall. **$90-$110** Right, **Sunburst gold vase,** 1950s, faint McCoy USA mark, 6" tall. **$60-$75**

Phial vase in dusty pink, mid-1980s, Designer Accents with USA and 44 mark, 12" wide. **$25-$30**

Non-production vase with carved leaves and branches, 1948, McCoy Made in USA mark with initials "TK," ex-Ty Kuhn collection, 8" tall. **No established value.**

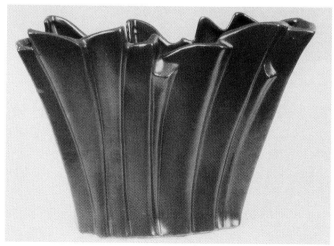

Large Fan vase, also called "Blades of Grass," glossy black, late 1950s, McCoy USA mark, 10" tall. **$175-$225**

Two Disc vases in glossy cobalt blue and burgundy, 1940s, also found in yellow and white, USA mark, 6 3/4" tall. **$100-$125 each**

Vases and Flower Holders

Five **Swan flower holders** in matte colors (called "ladder pieces," so named because they were pictured in a early McCoy guide on a drying rack that was tiered like the steps of a ladder), 1940s, NM USA mark, 3 1/4" tall. Usually **$60-$70,** but yellow and pink (the only one found in glossy finish) may bring **$100-$125**

Five **Pitcher flower holders,** 1940s, NM USA mark, 3 1/4" tall. In pink blue and yellow, **$80-$90** each; In coral and hand-painted, **$150-$200 each**

Six **Praying Hands flower holders**, 1940s, NM USA mark, 3" tall. **$100-$125 each** except for white and aqua, **$50-$60**

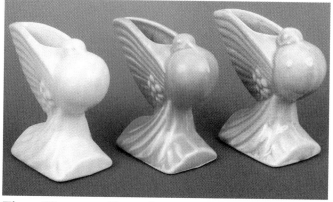

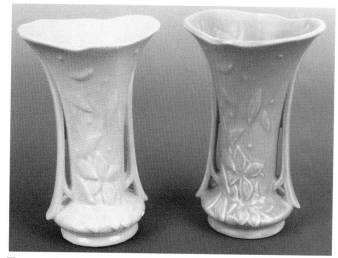

Three **Pigeon or Dove flower holders** (called "ladder pieces," so named because they were pictured in a early McCoy guide on a drying rack that was tiered like the steps of a ladder), 1940s, USA mark, 3 1/2" tall, 1940s. **$100-$125 each**

Two **vases** in matte yellow and aqua, 1940s, NM USA mark, also found in white, 8" tall. **$50-$60 each**

Six miniature **Cornucopia flower holders** in matte colors, 1940s, NM USA mark, 3 1/4" tall. Blue, white, aqua, **$50-$60**; Pink and yellow, **$125-$150**; Coral, **$175-$225**

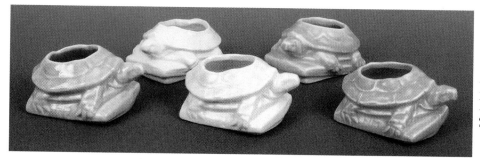

Five **Turtle flower holders** (also called miniature planters), 1940s, NM USA mark, 4 1/4" long. Aqua and white, **$40-$50**; Blue, **$70-$80**; Pink and yellow, **$125-$150 each**

Two **vases with leaves and stylized flowers** in glossy green and matte aqua, stoneware, late 1920s, unmarked, 7" tall. **$110-$125 each**

Vases and Flower Holders

Two **vases** in matte aqua, 1940s, unmarked or USA mark, 9" tall. **$50-$60 each**

Left, **vase** in glossy aqua with hand-painted flowers, 1940s, McCoy mark, 8" tall. **$125-$150** because of painting; normally, **$60-$70** Right, **Cornucopia vase** in glossy aqua, 1940s, round McCoy mark, 7" tall. **$50-$60**

Left, **Hobnail and Leaves vase** in glossy aqua, 1940s, NM USA mark, 7" tall. **$75-$85** Right, **Ring ware vase with handles** in glossy green, 1940s, McCoy USA mark, 5 1/2" tall. **$50-$60**

Two **Basket-weave vases** in glossy aqua and green, 6" and 7". **$45-$55 each**

Four 5" **Basket-weave vases** in glossy burgundy, green, white, and blue. **$40-$50 each**

Left, **Fluted vase** with zigzag top in glossy aqua, 1950s, McCoy USA mark, 10" tall (also found in 8 and 14" sizes). **$90-$110**
Right, **vase in glossy aqua,** 1940s, unmarked or NM mark, 8" tall. **$50-$60**

Two **vases in glossy aqua**. Left, 1940s, round McCoy mark, 9" tall. **$45-$55**
Right, **Square Cherry vase,** stoneware, 1930s, round McCoy mark, 12" tall. **$125-$150**

Left, **two-handled vase** in glossy aqua, 1940s, McCoy mark. **$50-$60** Right, **Uncle Sam vase** in glossy aqua, 1940s, incised McCoy mark, 7 1/2" tall, also found in yellow and white. **$60-$70** (Beware of reproductions, which may be slightly smaller.)

Left, **Sailboat vase** with square bottom in matte aqua, 1940s, NM USA or NM mark, other matte colors, 9" tall. **$85-$95**
Right, **two-handled vase** in matte aqua, 1940s, McCoy mark, other matte colors, 9" tall. **$55-$65**

Three **vases in glossy aqua.**
Left, 8" tall, round McCoy USA
mark. **$25-$35** Center, 12" tall,
McCoy USA mark, also found
in yellow and white. **$50-$60**
Right, 7 1/2" tall, round McCoy
USA mark, found in other
colors. **$25-$35**

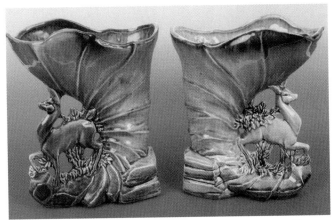

Two **Deer and Cornucopia vases,** 1950s, McCoy
USA mark, 9" tall, right example in rare brown and
green. Left, **$70-$80**; Right, **$125-$150**

Two **matte aqua vases,** 10" tall, found in other
matte colors. Left, unmarked, **$85-$95** Right, arrow
leaf, McCoy mark. **$125-$150**

Two **vases**, one with fired-on decoration (possibly a
lunch-hour piece), 1940s, USA mark, 10" tall. With
decoration, **$125-$150**; Without, **$75-$90**

Two **matte aqua vases,** 9" tall. Left, 1940s, McCoy
mark, found in both matte and glossy colors. **$55-
$65** Right, urn vase, 1940s, USA mark, rarely found
in other matte colors. **$75-$85**

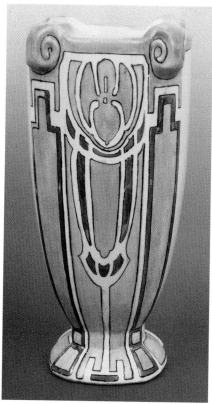

Vase with fired-on decoration, art nouveau influence similar to Brush-McCoy, 1920s, unmarked, 8" tall. **$450-$500**

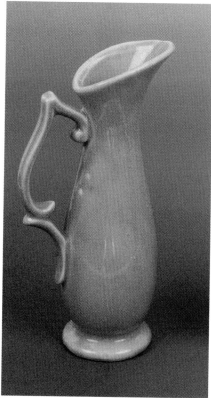

Pitcher vase, 1950s, McCoy USA mark, 7 1/2" tall. **$25-$35**

Tall Scroll vase in matte green (often found in glossy tan-brown), late 1940s, USA mark, 14" tall. **$150-$200**

Two **matte aqua vases,** 10" and 11 1/2" tall. Left, 1940s, USA mark, **$85-$9 5** Right, 1930s, unmarked, Stoneware. **$150-$175** Also found in sizes ranging from 6" to18".

Two **matte aqua vases,** 12" tall. Left, 1940s, NM mark, frequently found with spots of other glazes, commonly cobalt blue. **$150-$175** Right, strap vase, usually found in glossy colors. **$175-$225**

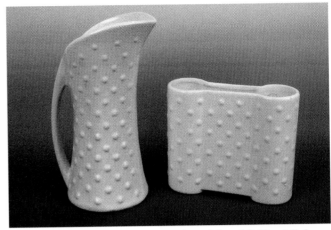

Left, **Hobnail "V" vase** in matte lavender, 1940s, NM USA mark, 9" tall. **$110-$125** Center and right, two **Hobnail vases** in matte aqua, 6" and 8", 1940s, NM USA mark. 6", **$55-$65**; 8", **$90-$110**

Left, **Hobnail pitcher vase** in white, 1940s, NM USA Mark, 10" tall. **$125-$150** Right, **Hobnail Castle Gate or "Binoculars" vase** in white, 1940s, unmarked, 6" tall. **$175-$200**

Two **matte aqua vases,** 8 1/2" and 10" Left, 1940s, round McCoy USA mark, found in matte and glossy colors. **$65-$75** Right, 1940s, McCoy mark, other matte colors. **$65-$75**

Two **matte aqua floor vases,** 14" tall: left, rib or fin vase, 1930s, unmarked, matte colors or drip glazes. **$500+** Right, **Sand Dollar vase**, 1930s and '40s, unmarked, matte or glossy colors. **$250-$300**

Two **matte aqua vases,** 8" and 7" Left, Tulip vase, 1940s, USA mark, matte and glossy colors. **$75-$85** Right, **Leafy vase,** found in matte colors, 1940s, unmarked. **$150-$175**

Two **matte aqua vases,** 9" and 7" Left, Swan vase, 1940s, McCoy mark. **$55-$65** Right, Cornucopia vase, 1940s, McCoy mark, **$45-$55**

Vases and Flower Holders

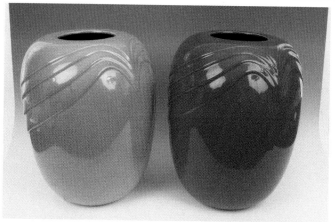

Two **Phial vases** in lavender and blue, mid-1980s, Designer Accents, marked 458 and USA, 12" tall. **$45-$50 each**

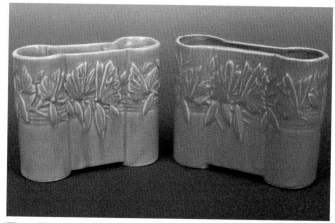

Two **Butterfly Line Castle Gate or "Binoculars" vases,** 1940s, USA mark or unmarked, found in other matte colors, 6" tall. **$185-$215 each**

Two **Butterfly Line vases**. Left, matte blue pitcher, 1940s, NM USA mark, 10" tall. **$175-$200** Right, cylinder vase in matte aqua, 1940s, NM USA mark, 6" tall. **$55-$65**

Left, **two-handled vase** in matte aqua, 1940s, unmarked, 6 1/2" tall. **$55-$65** Right, **vase in glossy yellow** (also found in burgundy and blue), 1940s, round McCoy mark, 8" tall. **$60-$70**

Floor vase in matte aqua, stoneware, 1930s or '40s, unmarked, matte and glossy colors, 18" tall. **$1,200+** (rare this size)

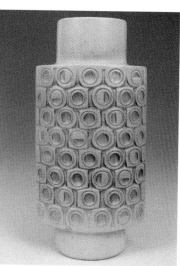

Scandia Line floor vase, 1970s, McCoy LCC mark, 14 1/2" tall. **$45-$55**

Vase (collectors call this the "Shrimp vase" because of its normal coloration) with applied maple leaves in atypical blue-black and yellow glaze (usually in chartreuse or salmon with green leaves), 1950s, McCoy USA mark, 9" tall. As shown, **$600+;** In common colors, **$175-$225**

Garden Club vase in matte yellow, late 1950s, McCoy USA mark, 9 1/2" tall. **$150-$175**

A grouping of what collectors call the **"5 in." vases** (though actual sizes vary by up to half an inch). Many vase styles are hard to find this size, and so this has become an entire collecting category. They are unmarked. Prices vary from about **$60** to more than **$125** depending on style, glaze, and mold quality, and how badly a collector needs one to complete a set.

Pitcher vase, 1970s (later version of a 1940s piece), USA mark or unmarked, 5" tall. **$25-$35**

Lily **Bud pillow vase** in matte aqua, 1940s, NM USA mark, 6 1/2" tall. **$75-$85**

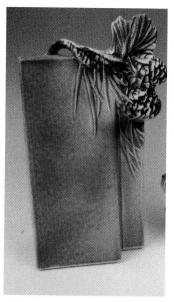

Pine cone vase, not a production piece, mid-1940s, McCoy USA mark, 9 1/2" tall. **$800-$1,000**

Rope-handle pitcher vase in matte aqua, late 1930s, unmarked, 7" tall. **$55-$65** Right, **Cornucopia vase** in matte aqua, 1940s, unmarked, 5 1/2" tall. **$55-$65**

Arcature vase in atypical dark lavender glaze (usually green and yellow), early 1950s, McCoy USA mark, 6 3/4" tall. In normal colors, **$50-$60**; As shown, **$150-$200**

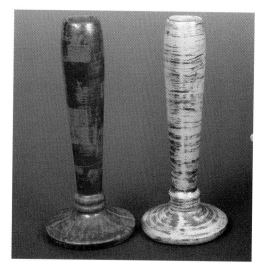

Classic Line bud vases, early 1960s, McCoy USA mark, 8" tall. **$35-$45 each**

Hand vase with separated fingers and painted nails, 1950s, NM USA mark, 6 1/2" tall. **$125-$150**

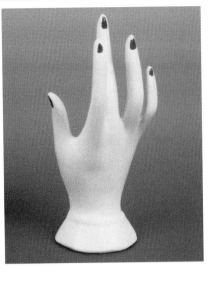

Ring ware vase in glossy burgundy, 1920s, unmarked, 9 1/4" tall. **$100-$125**

Lily Bud pillow vase in glossy rose/pink, 1940s, NM USA mark, 7" tall. **$90-$110**

Sunflower vase using same mold as lamp, 1950s, with unusual air-brush decoration, unmarked. **$450-$550**

Grecian urn vase, 9 1/2" tall, 1950s. **$110-$125**

Ribbed vase in atypical brown glaze, 1940s, unmarked, 6 1/2" tall. **$55-$65**

Vases

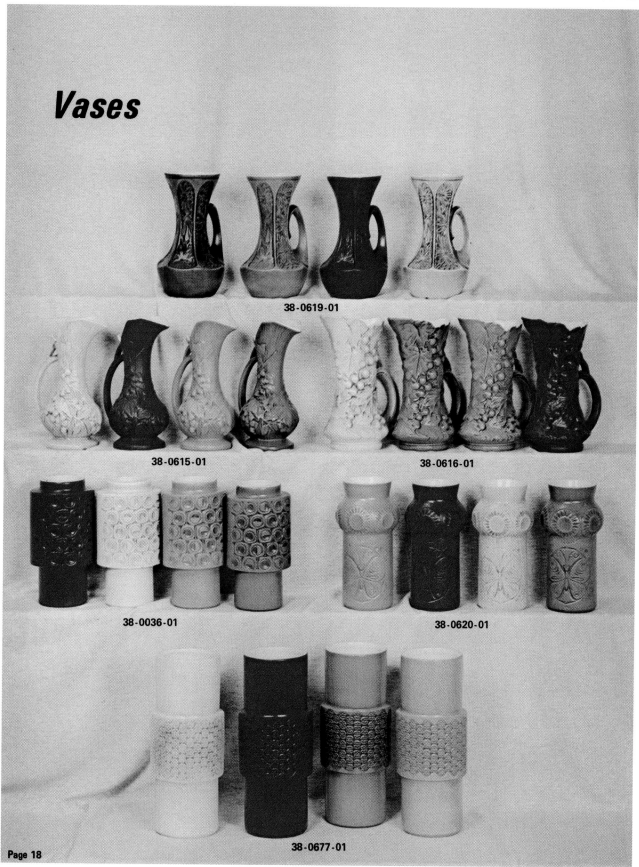

38-0619-01

38-0615-01   38-0616-01

38-0036-01   38-0620-01

38-0677-01

Page 18

Vases in several styles were featured in a 1975 Nelson McCoy catalog.

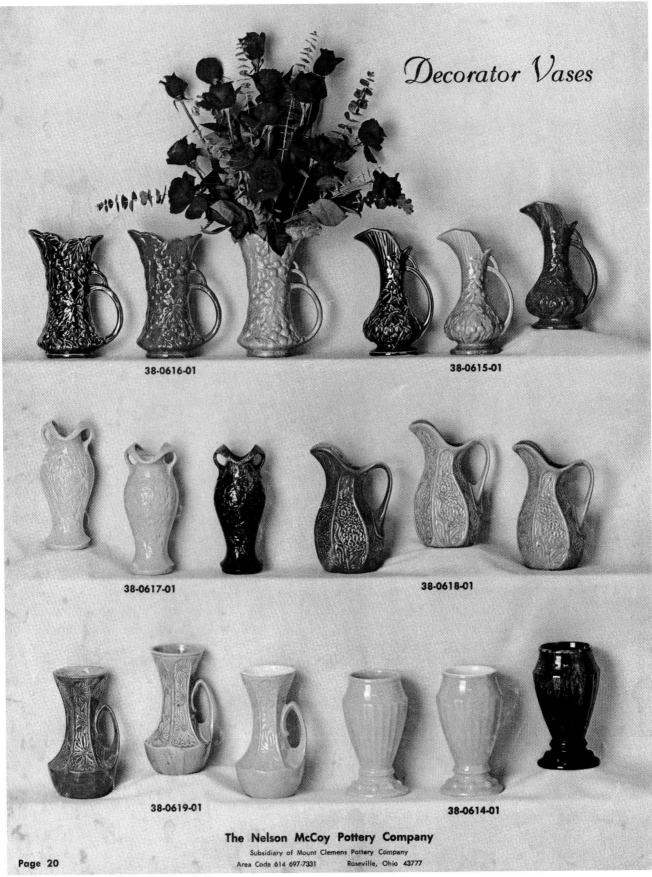

Decorator Vases

38-0616-01 38-0615-01

38-0617-01 38-0618-01

38-0619-01 38-0614-01

The Nelson McCoy Pottery Company
Subsidiary of Mount Clemens Pottery Company
Area Code 614 697-7331 Roseville, Ohio 43777

A page of Decorator Vases was included in a McCoy catalog.

Wall Pockets

Wall pockets by nature are easily damaged, so collectors should look for signs of restoration around chipped holes and on high points, and paint touch-ups on those made with cold-paint decoration. Examples in gold trim command a higher price.

Apple wall pocket in gold trim, 1950s, unmarked, 7" long. **$200-$225**

Bananas wall pocket, green leaves, with gold trim, 1950s, unmarked, 7" long. **$400-$450**

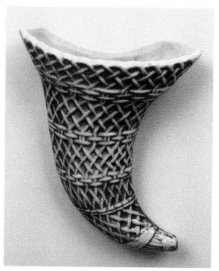

Basket-weave Horn of Plenty wall pocket, 1950s, McCoy USA mark, 8" long. **$100-$120**

Blossomtime wall pocket in matte yellow, McCoy mark, 7 3/4" long. **$90-$110**

Blossomtime wall pocket in matte white, McCoy mark, 7 3/4" long. **$90-$110**

Butterfly wall pocket in matte aqua with crisp mold, 1940s, NM mark, 6" tall. **$450-$550**

Wall Pockets

Clown or Jester wall pocket with cold-paint decoration, 1940s, McCoy mark, 8 1/2" long. **$90-$110,** depending on paint condition

Cuckoo Clock wall pocket in gold trim (comes with both Roman and Arabic numerals, and in a range of colors), 1950s, McCoy mark, 8" tall without weights. **$200-$225**

Grapes wall pocket in gold trim, 1950s, unmarked, 7" long. **$300-$350**

Fan wall pocket in gold Brocade, found in other colors and gold trimmed, 1950s, McCoy USA and 24 kt. gold marks, 8 1/2" wide. **$85-$95**

Iron on a Trivet wall pocket, 1950s, McCoy USA, 8" long. **$85-$95**

Three Flower form wall pockets, late 1940s, unmarked, 6" tall. The blue and coral are common colors, **$40-$50**; Center, with under-glaze decoration, **$175-$225**

Lily wall pocket in yellow, McCoy mark, 6 1/2" long. **$80-$100**

Fancy Lily Bud wall pocket in matte aqua, 1940s, incised McCoy mark, 8" long. **$225-$250**

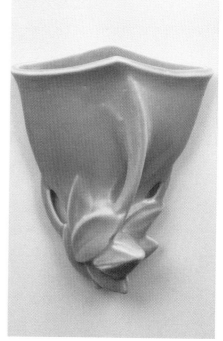

Large Lily Bud wall pocket in matte aqua, 1940s, NM USA mark, 8" long. **$150-$175**

Small Lily Bud wall pocket in matte aqua, 1940s, NM USA mark, 6" long. **$65-$75**

Lady in the Bonnet wall pocket with cold-paint decoration, 1940s, McCoy mark, wide variety of paint colors and details, 8" long. **$70-$80**

Lovebirds on a Trivet wall pocket, 1950s, McCoy USA mark, 8" long. **$75-$85**

Mailbox wall pocket, early 1950s, McCoy USA mark, also found with cold-paint decoration. **$90-$110** (beware of reproductions in bright pastels)

Mexican Man wall pocket in matte aqua, 1940s, NM USA mark, 7 1/2" long. **$65-$75**

Owls on a Trivet wall pocket with some cold-paint decoration, 1950s, McCoy USA mark, 8" long. **$75-$85**

Pear wall pocket in gold trim, 1950s, unmarked, 7" long. **$200-$225**

Umbrella wall pocket, 1950s, McCoy USA mark, found in other colors including gold Brocade Line, 8 1/4" long. **$75-$85**

Urn wall pocket in speckled pink glaze with gold trim, McCoy USA mark, also found in chartreuse, 4 1/2" long. **$75-$85**

Violin wall pocket in blue with gold trim, 1950s, McCoy USA and Shafer mark, 10" long. **$275-$325**

Violin wall pocket in black, a hard to find color. **$350-$400**

A collection of **Fruit wall pockets**, and the corresponding fruit planters.

Catalog Covers

Nelson McCoy Pottery Company 1979

**Nelson McCoy
For 1975**

Nelson McCoy Pottery Company
SUBSIDIARY OF LANCASTER COLONY CORPORATION
ROSEVILLE, OHIO 43777

The Nelson McCoy Pottery Company

Area Code 614 697-7331   Roseville, Ohio 43777

1966

introducing
McCoy for '73

The Nelson McCoy Pottery Company
Roseville, Ohio 43777

GIVE A HOOT
DON'T POLLUTE
WOODSY OWL

McCoy for `72

The Nelson McCoy Pottery Company
Subsidiary of Mount Clemens China Company
Roseville, Ohio 43777